# DARK HORSES

## JUMPS GUIDE 2011–2012

# DARK HORSES
## JUMPS GUIDE 2011–2012

Marten Julian

Published in 2001 by Raceform
Compton, Newbury, Berkshire, RG20 6NL

A catalogue record for this book is available from the British Library.

ISBN 978-1-906820-82-4

Designed by Fiona Pike

Printed in the UK by CPI William Clowes Beccles NR34 7TL

# CONTENTS

# Keep in touch

If you want to keep in touch with Marten's thoughts on a regular basis then read his free-to-view journal at:

## www.martenjulian.com

or ring him on:

# 0906 150 1555

Selections given in the first minute

(Calls charged at £1.50 a minute at all times and may cost more from a mobile)

## Follow Marten

 @martenjulian

# INTRODUCTION

Thank you for buying the 2011-12 edition of the *Dark Horses Jumps Guide*. I hope that you find the book a useful source of reference through the course of the season.

I am, as always, hopeful for the 20 horses which I have nominated for the Premier List this time around. The list includes a few horses from low-profile yards in the hope that they will represent good value for betting purposes when they appear.

There are also sections devoted to Dark Horses, drawn from a variety of sources including France and the point-to-point world, while the Handicap Projects include horses which left the impression last season they were being campaigned with long-term objectives in mind. I advise you to monitor the market carefully when they appear.

I hope you enjoy reading the essays on the Gold Cup, Champion Hurdle and Queen Mother Champion Chase. Given the dominance of Big Buck's in the staying hurdle division I decided to write instead about the contenders for the Queen Mother Champion Chase.

Ladbrokes have again kindly agreed to back the Trainers' Selections feature. A sum of £2 for every level stake point profit made by any horse in the feature will be paid to the Injured Jockeys' Fund. I am grateful to all the trainers who got back to us with names of dark or unexposed horses and, in particular, my daughter Rebecca for bringing the project together.

I would like to thank James de Wesselow, Julian Brown, Anthony Bromley, Rebecca Dixon, Jodie Standing, Steve Dixon, Alex Julian, Paul Day, Mike Dillon and Richard Lowther for their help at various stages of the book.

If you wish to keep updated with my news and information on the featured horses then refer to the free-to-view journal on my website (www.martenjulian.com).

Alternatively you can hear my news on a daily basis, when special reference is usually given to the horses included in this book, on 0906 150 1555 (calls cost £1.50 a minute at all times). Any selections are always given within the first minute of the message.

Please contact Rebecca Dixon if you would details of my services for the current campaign (rebecca@martenjulian.com) or call us on 01539 741007.

Finally, it only remains for me to wish you the best of good fortune in the weeks ahead.

Bye for now

Marten

# THE PREMIER LIST

The following horses, which come from a variety of backgrounds, are selected in the hope and belief that they will collectively reward support to level stakes. You can keep updated on a regular basis with my thoughts on their progress by calling my line (see elsewhere)

## Alexander Road (6yr Bay Mare)

**Trainer:** Donald McCain
**Pedigree:** Kaldounevees – Trinity Belle (Tel Quel)
**Form:** 034111P -
**Chase Rating:** —
**Hurdle Rating:** 128
**Optimum Trip:** 3m

Very likeable mare, who thrived for the step up in trip when winning novices' hurdles at Carlisle and Sedgefield, both over 2m 4f, and then back at Carlisle over 3m 1f before pulling up when over the top on her final start in a handicap hurdle at Ayr (128).

Ridden prominently to win her races, battling on strongly in the closing stages, and has right credentials to develop into a very useful staying chaser.

Has a tremendous attitude and looks an ideal type for mares only novice chases. Relishes a stiff track and soft ground, so one to keep on side in the depths of midwinter.

Al Ferof, likely to take high rank as a novice chaser

# Al Ferof (6yr Grey Gelding)

| | |
|---|---|
| **Trainer:** | Paul Nicholls |
| **Pedigree:** | Dom Alco – Maralta (Altayan) |
| **Form:** | 3112/F3111 - |
| **Chase Rating:** | — |
| **Hurdle Rating:** | 154 |
| **Optimum Trip:** | 2m 4f |

Fell on his point-to-point debut then won at Athlacca in May, 2009. Shaped well when finishing third and winning from two runs in bumpers for former handler Elizabeth Doyle and subsequently sold to John Hales, for whom he made a winning debut in a Newbury bumper in February, 2010. Next time ran well to chase home Cue Card in the Weatherbys Champion Bumper at Cheltenham in March.

Fell on his hurdling debut at Cheltenham last December and then third to Backspin in Challow Hurdle at Newbury later that month. Dropped in class to win extended 2m 3f novices' hurdle at Taunton in January and again ran out an easy winner when beating Oasis Knight by 15 lengths at Newbury in February.

Showed significant improvement a month later at Cheltenham, coming with a strong run from off the pace to beat Spirit Son by two lengths in the Supreme Novices' Hurdle at Cheltenham.

Proved well suited to the strong pace at Cheltenham, suggesting he will benefit considerably from a step up to two and a half miles.

Likely to be trained for the Arkle Trophy (currently 14/1), a race suited to horses which appreciate trips beyond two miles. Has the potential to become a Gold Cup horse one day.

## Arctic Court (7yr Bay Gelding)

| | |
|---|---|
| **Trainer:** | Jim Goldie |
| **Pedigree:** | Arctic Lord – Polls Joy (Pollerton) |
| **Form:** | 4000/201P231 - 22 |
| **Chase Rating:** | — |
| **Hurdle Rating:** | 130 |
| **Optimum Trip:** | 3m + |

Has always hinted at something more than he has shown, notably early in his career in bumpers and novice hurdles over inadequate trips, and duly improved when stepped up in distance winning an extended 3m 0-115 handicap hurdle at Ayr in January going away by three and three-quarter lengths (110).

Pulled up next time at Huntingdon, but then ran well in his four remaining outings in the spring, winning, finishing second twice and third once. Started the new season on a mark of 130 and has the potential to become a useful staying chaser.

Half-brother to 3m chase winner Into The Clan and other stayers, from the family of Keen Leader.

Owner Raymond Anderson Green places his horses with great skill, so keep this one in mind for a decent staying handicap, possibly at Ayr.

## Barney Cool (4yr Bay Gelding)

| | |
|---|---|
| **Trainer:** | David Pipe |
| **Pedigree:** | Bollin Eric – Laurel Diver (Celtic Cone) |
| **Form:** | 1 |
| **Chase Rating:** | — |
| **Hurdle Rating:** | — |
| **Optimum Trip:** | 2m + |

Justified strong market support (backed to 4/7) when producing a useful turn of foot to beat Dark Shadow in a 1m 6f bumper at Fontwell in May. Fine effort in view of his stout pedigree and the tightness of the track.

By St Leger winner Bollin Eric out of a bumper-winning sister to a 2m 4f chaser, by Celtic Cone, a very strong influence for stamina. This horse is a half-brother to the useful staying hurdle/chaser Mr Cool, 2m 6f winner Miss Cool, 3m winner Very Cool and others.

Must be useful to have won over 1m 6f at a track as sharp as Fontwell. Definitely one to keep on the right side.

## Burton Port (7yr Bay Gelding)

**Trainer:**　　　　Nicky Henderson
**Pedigree:**　　　Bob Back – Despute (Be My Native)
**Form:**　　　　　113342/1211121/2 -
**Chase Rating:**　166
**Hurdle Rating:**　150
**Optimum Trip:**　3m

*Bob Back – the sire of so many top jumpers including Burton Port*

Extremely game and consistent performer, who has only once finished out of the first three in 14 outings over hurdles and fences.

Shaped extremely well when second to Diamond Harry in the Hennessy Gold Cup on his seasonal debut, staying on with the utmost tenacity at the finish despite having lost momentum with mistakes in the final mile.

Had surprised his trainer with his rate of improvement the season before, winning a modest beginners' chase at Bangor in November and then again at Lingfield, Southwell and Ascot before chasing home Weapon's Amnesty in the RSA Chase. Improved again a month later when beating Dance Island in the Mildmay Novices' Chase over 3m 1f, staying on strongly for firm driving to win by three and a quarter lengths.

Had proved himself a useful performer over hurdles, running progressively better as he was stepped up in trip.

Sustained a tendon injury after the Hennessy but is expected to return at some point this season and may be good enough to warrant a crack at the Gold Cup. Was fancied as a long-term prospect for that race last autumn and is currently rated 16lb behind Long Run.

A thoroughly likeable horse who, at the age of seven, still has youth on his side.

## Buy Back Bob (4yr Chestnut Gelding)

| | |
|---|---|
| **Trainer:** | Tony Martin |
| **Pedigree:** | Big Bad Bob – Abeyr (Unfuwain) |
| **Form:** | 3 |
| **Chase Rating:** | — |
| **Hurdle Rating:** | — |
| **Optimum Trip:** | 2m |

Unexposed over hurdles but has shown plenty of ability on the Flat, notably for former trainer Ger Lyons, winning over a mile at Dundalk on the second of his two starts at two and then once from six starts at three, winning a 1m 2f EBF contest at Navan in June, 2010. Beaten off 93 and 93 on last two starts that season and subsequently sold for £140,000 to Patsy Byrne at Tattersalls in October, 2010.

Ran for his new connections for the first time over hurdles at Cork in August this year, finishing third of 22 to Rebel Fitz before finishing down the field in a 1m handicap on the Flat at Gowran Park a month later. Shaped very well over hurdles, held on inside and making headway approaching home turn. Jumped deliberately second last and at last, losing footing on landing, but kept on well to the line.

Quietly supported at long odds for Cesarewitch and ran better than finishing position suggests, creeping into contention half a mile from home before fading in the closing stages to finish 12th of 33.

Was bought for a lot of money by an owner who likes a tilt at the ring, so highly probable that he will be the subject of strong market interest at some point. Has plenty of size and scope (impressed in the paddock at Newmarket) and showed enough at Cork to suggest he can win any run-of-the-mill novice event.

## Cucumber Run (6yr Bay Gelding)

| | |
|---|---|
| **Trainer:** | Nicky Henderson |
| **Pedigree:** | Oscar – Back To Roost (Presenting) |
| **Form:** | 221/02110 - |
| **Chase Rating:** | — |
| **Hurdle Rating:** | 131 |
| **Optimum Trip:** | 2m + |

Trainer has always rated this half-brother to Somersby highly but despite winning three races he has not quite lived up to expectations.

Beaten favourite, at 4/7 and 6/5, on his first two starts in bumpers but made amends next time at Kempton, racing awkwardly but staying on to win going away.

Highly tried on hurdling debut in Listed extended 2m hurdle at Cheltenham, shaping quite well to finish fifth to Rock On Ruby. Beaten three-quarters of a length by Pride In Battle in 2m 3f contest next time at Newbury before winning modest events at Huntingdon and Hereford. Not at his best when down the field in the EBF Novices' Handicap Hurdle on his final start at Sandown (132).

Has not really done much wrong apart from that last outing. Expected to continue over hurdles for a while, perhaps sticking at two and a half miles, before consideration is given to a switch to chasing.

## Dare Me (7yr Bay Gelding)

**Trainer:** Philip Hobbs
**Pedigree:** Bob Back – Gaye Chatelaine (Castle Keep)
**Form:** 1/102/11 -
**Chase Rating:** —
**Hurdle Rating:** 140
**Optimum Trip:** 2m

Very well-regarded son of lightly-raced mare from the family of Gaye Brief, Gaye Chance, Kingsmark and Simon.

Has always shown ability, winning a bumper at Haydock on his racecourse debut in November, 2008, but then off until February, 2010, when he won another bumper at Ffos Las (raced keenly).

Ran well behind Cue Card in Weatherbys Champion Bumper at Cheltenham but put up a better effort when beaten one and a half lengths by Megastar in the Grade 2 bumper at Aintree.

Returned last autumn to win modest novice hurdles at Exeter but then injured a hind leg and had to miss the remainder of the season. Expected to tackle handicap hurdles before switching to fences.

Entitled to stay further than two miles but can be keen and does not lack speed, so may be suited to a strongly-run race over the minimum trip. Classy.

## Diocles (5yr Bay Gelding)

| | |
|---|---|
| **Trainer:** | Donald McCain |
| **Pedigree:** | Bob Back – Ardrina (Ardross) |
| **Form:** | 1 - |
| **Chase Rating:** | — |
| **Hurdle Rating:** | — |
| **Optimum Trip:** | 2m + |

Appeared to win only a modest bumper at Southwell in December, but form could not have worked out better with the second, fourth, fifth (beaten 29 lengths) and sixth (beaten 40 lengths) going on to prove subsequent winners.

Won in most impressive fashion, responding to the gentlest encouragement to quicken eight lengths clear of Bunclody, subsequently acquired by this trainer from his former handler.

Comes from a very stout female line – dam stayed 3m 2f and is related to smart bumper winner and 2m to 2m 5f hurdle winner Mendo – but showed at Southwell that he has loads of speed.

Missed the rest of the season after sustaining a small hairline fracture to his cannon bone. Looks a horse of great potential and did well to win over such a sharp two miles given his stamina-laden pedigree.

## Fourth Estate (5yr Bay Gelding)

| | |
|---|---|
| **Trainer:** | Nicky Henderson |
| **Pedigree:** | Fantastic Light – Papering (Shaadi) |
| **Form:** | 11 - |
| **Chase Rating:** | — |
| **Hurdle Rating:** | — |
| **Optimum Trip:** | 2m |

Probably one of the most impressive bumpers winners from last season, staying on well to win cosily from subsequent Flat winner Harvey's Hope on his debut at

Doncaster and then again when beating Toubeera on a tight rein, and under a penalty, in the Ashleybank Open National Hunt Flat Race at Ayr in April.

Trainer likes to target that Ayr race – he won it the previous season with Sprinter Sacre – and every chance this half-brother to Listed winner Dossier and close relative of 2m hurdle winner Prima Vista will attain similar heights.

Set to go novice hurdling and has the potential to go a long way. Classy and very promising.

## James De Vassy (6yr Bay Gelding)

**Trainer:** Nick Williams
**Pedigree:** Lavirco – Provenchere (Son Of Silver)
**Form:** 104/1423/01 -
**Chase Rating:** —
**Hurdle Rating:** 151
**Optimum Trip:** 2m 4f

*Nick Williams, one of the game's shrewdest trainers*

Has been handled with great care and skill by his trainer, winning on his racecourse debut at Wincanton in January, 2009, and ending the season with an eye-catching effort in a novices' hurdle at Warwick.

Started the 2009/10 campaign on 120 and duly won an extended 2m limited handicap hurdle at Chepstow by four lengths despite being 4lb out of the handicap (124). Not disgraced next time when fourth of 15 to Khyber Kim in valuable Greatwood Handicap at Cheltenham and then second to well-regarded Royal Charm in limited handicap on heavy ground at Exeter in December.

Rested until the 2010 Cheltenham Festival, he ran very well to finish third of 28 to Spirit River in the Coral Cup (143) battling on well from the second last. Disappointing on his return to action at Haydock last November, he returned to winning form when beating Organisateur by two lengths in the 2m 5f Lanzarote Hurdle at Kempton in January (144).

Loves soft ground but may be best at trips up to around two and a half miles. Has risen 27lb since switched to handicap hurdling and has the ability to develop into a top-notch chaser.

## Kid Cassidy (5yr Bay Gelding)

**Trainer:** Nicky Henderson
**Pedigree:** Beneficial – Shuil Na Lee (Phardante)
**Form:** 13/132 - 1
**Chase Rating:** —
**Hurdle Rating:** 144
**Optimum Trip:** 2m

Has always been very well regarded, by both the trainer and jockey AP McCoy, but has not really built on his early promise.

Made a winning racecourse debut in an extended 1m 4f bumper at Newbury in March, 2010, and then finished third of 23 to Bishopsfurze in a bumper at Punchestown in April.

Returned to action the following autumn with a 15-lengths defeat of the useful Tornado Bob in a Class 3 maiden hurdle at Newbury after being hampered at the second last. Next time out, back at Newbury, he ran third to useful performers Rock On Ruby and Megastar having pulled hard in the early stages of the race.

Was withdrawn at the start after appearing distressed due the incident where two horses were electrocuted at Newbury on his next outing and may still have been feeling the effects of that when reluctant to go to post (ponied to the start) at Sandown in February, running second to Hildisvini.

Gave more indication of his potential on his final start in a fair novice hurdle at Punchestown in May, beating useful performer Celtic Folklore by 13 lengths without coming off the bridle, with 124-rated horse the best part of a further 12 lengths back in fourth.

Half-brother to four winners including River City out of an unraced mare from the family of Welsh National winner Jocks Cross.

Rated a high-class prospect and may contest a valuable handicap before being asked to take a further step up in grade. This could be a very good season for him.

## Reve De Sivola (6yr Bay Gelding)

| | |
|---|---|
| **Trainer:** | Nick Williams |
| **Pedigree:** | Assessor – Eva De Chalamont (Iron Duke) |
| **Form:** | 12121/413033 - 40 |
| **Chase Rating:** | 141 |
| **Hurdle Rating:** | 148 |
| **Optimum Trip:** | 3m + |

Generally disappointing last season, beating Wishfull Thinking by one and a quarter lengths in a 2m 5f novices' chase at Cheltenham (rec. 8lb) but then failed to progress from that, beaten a long way by Hell's Bay over the same course and distance next time out and again by Medermit in the Scilly Isles Novices' Chase at Sandown.

Shaped better when fair third to Bensalem, equipped for the first time with cheekpieces and jumping carelessly, in an extended 3m handicap at the Cheltenham Festival (140). Ran well again next time at Aintree, looking likely to win 3m 1f Listed contest until jumping to the right at last when in the lead and finishing third. Ran a fair race when fourth to 150-rated Quito De La Roque on his next start

*Reve De Sivola, who may not have been quite as his best last season*

in 3m 1f Grade 1 novice chase at Punchestown, again making clumsy errors.

Had promised so much more as a hurdler, shaping well as a novice (sixth to Zaynar in Triumph Hurdle) and improved again in 2009/10 season, winning three times and second twice from five starts, notably when beating Restless Harry and Finian's Rainbow in Grade 1 Challow Hurdle before chasing home Peddlers Cross in the Neptune Hurdle at Cheltenham. Put up a career-best effort when showing the utmost tenacity to win the Grade 1 Cathal Ryan Memorial Champion Novice Hurdle at Punchestown in April, 2010, after being squeezed out and losing many lengths on the turn for home.

Was rated a potential Gold Cup prospect in his younger days but, at six, is still young enough to progress beyond last season's form. Looks the right type for one of the season's top staying handicap chases.

Worth another chance to fulfil his early promise. Still reasonably treated over fences, 7lb below his rating over hurdles.

# Rock On Ruby (6yr Bay Gelding)

| | |
|---|---|
| **Trainer:** | Paul Nicholls |
| **Pedigree:** | Oscar – Stony View (Tirol) |
| **Form:** | 411/11223 - |
| **Chase Rating:** | — |
| **Hurdle Rating:** | 145 |
| **Optimum Trip:** | 2m 4f |

Has a very likeable way of going and has not finished out of the first three since his bumper debut at Newbury in November, 2009.

Won bumpers on his next three starts, at Taunton, Newbury and Cheltenham and made a winning hurdling debut back at Newbury in December, beating Megastar by six lengths. Stepped up again when running Bobs Worth to two and a quarter lengths in Grade 2 contest over an extended 2m 4f at Cheltenham and then unlucky to be beaten a short head by First Lieutenant over the same course and distance in the Grade 1 Neptune Novices' Hurdle at the Festival in March, just touched off on the line.

Failed to reproduce that form in a Grade 2 contest next time at Aintree, finishing 21 lengths third to Spirit Son.

Showed great courage and tenacity last season and looks an ideal horse to follow, whatever the level. Not sure to stay three miles on pedigree and may be best around 2m 4f or even back to two miles for the time being.

# Royal Charm (6yr Black Gelding)

**Trainer:** Paul Nicholls
**Pedigree:** Cadoudal – Victoria Royale (Garde Royale)
**Form:** 22/113/113 -
**Chase Rating:** 145
**Hurdle Rating:** 145
**Optimum Trip:** 2m +

Possibly flattered by his consistent form figures because he has not yet realised the high hopes held for him by his trainer.

Shaped well on both starts in 2008-09 and won his first two starts in good style that autumn, on heavy ground at Exeter in November and then back at the track a month later, beating James De Vassy by eight lengths (137). Beaten next time in Grade 2 contest at Cheltenham by Restless Harry, possibly finding the extended 2m 4f trip beyond him.

Impressed on seasonal debut on return to action last November, winning an extended 2m 1f beginners' chase by 22 lengths, before beating Leo's Lucky Star over the same course and distance a month later. Was put away until reappearing at Aintree in April in a Grade 2 novices' chase, running well until hitting the fifth last. Not punished thereafter and allowed to come home in his own time. Trainer reported afterwards the ground was probably too quick for him.

Leaves the impression he has a touch of class, and could be the right type for a top handicap. Optimum trip uncertain, but will probably stay two and a half miles.

## Salut Flo (6yr Bay Gelding)

| | |
|---|---|
| **Trainer:** | David Pipe |
| **Pedigree:** | Saint Des Saints – Royale Marie (Garde Royale) |
| **Form:** | 003013/10028112/ |
| **Chase Rating:** | 137 |
| **Hurdle Rating:** | 137 |
| **Optimum Trip:** | 2m 4f |

*Salut Flo, who could make giant strides this season*

A decent performer in France, who won twice over hurdles at Auteuil and a 2m 3f chase at Cagnes-Sur-Mer in January, 2010, before joining this trainer.

Was rated on 118 for his UK chasing debut and won with any amount in hand, always up with the pace despite brushing through the top of a few of the fences in a 2m 3f 0-125 handicap chase at Doncaster. Was raised a stone, to 132, and again ran a game second to Prince De Beauchene in a 2m 4f handicap chase at Haydock )heavy ground), battling on bravely for one so inexperienced after being headed (Mister McGoldrick 24 lengths back in third).

Was entered for decent handicaps during that spring, indicating the high regard in which he is held, but had to miss last season due to leg trouble. Now rated on 137 but still unexposed and looks just the right type for a valuable handicap chase. Has youth on his side and may still be a few pounds ahead of the handicapper.

An exciting prospect who could not be in better hands.

## Sona Sasta (8yr Bay Gelding)

**Trainer:** David Pipe
**Pedigree:** Sonus – Derry Lark (Lancastrian)
**Form:** 004/0110/110 -
**Chase Rating:** 128
**Hurdle Rating:** 106
**Optimum Trip:** 3m +

Won, second and third from three starts in Irish point-to-points and given three runs in novice and maiden company over hurdles at Taunton, very much with handicaps in mind.

Disappointing in 3m 1f 0-105 on handicap debut in December, 2009, from a mark of 93 but did better a month later when winning a similar event at Ffos Las by four lengths from Hopeful Star. Defied a 10lb higher mark a fortnight later at Huntingdon but beaten on his final outing of the season in 3m 0-120 handicap hurdle at Cheltenham.

Reappeared last season in January, easily winning a 3m handicap chase at Taunton by 18 lengths from a mark of 106, and followed up under a 7lb penalty in a similar

*Sona Sasta – an ideal type for one of the season's top staying handicap chases*

race at Newbury (113). Ran a better race than his finishing position would suggest on his final start in the 4m National Hunt Chase at Cheltenham, meeting most of his rivals on highly unfavourable terms (23lb wrong with the winner) and coming home in sixth on ground which would not have been as soft he likes.

Still favourably treated on a mark of 128 and looks an ideal type for a long-distance handicap chase in the mud. One to bear in mind for the Welsh National or similar sort of race.

## Top It All (8yr Bay Gelding)

| | |
|---|---|
| **Trainer:** | Rose Dobbin |
| **Pedigree:** | Beat All – Forever Shineing (Glint Of Gold) |
| **Form:** | 0400020/P03142 - |
| **Chase Rating:** | 104 |
| **Hurdle Rating:** | 97 |
| **Optimum Trip:** | 3m |

Not as exposed as his age would imply, having run just 13 times and been brought along quietly in his early races.

Showed significant improvement when switched to fences last season, finishing third in a 3m 1f novices' handicap chase at Kelso (95) and then winning over an extended 2m 6f at the same track just over a fortnight later. Didn't jump well next time at Catterick (100) but returned to form on final start in January, running second to Eyre Square over 3m1f (100).

*Rose Dobbin (in silks), trainer of the promising Top It All*

Has run just four times over fences and definitely capable of improvement. Just the type his owner likes to aim at a top staying handicap chase, perhaps with the Scottish National as a long-term objective.

## Tornado Bob (6yr Brown Gelding)

**Trainer:** Donald McCain
**Pedigree:** Bob Back – Double Glazed (Glacial Storm)
**Form:** 30/12112P -
**Chase Rating:** —
**Hurdle Rating:** 143
**Optimum Trip:** 2m 4f +

A favourite from last season, who was possibly unlucky not to beat Sonofvic at Ascot in February after ploughing through the last flight of hurdles.

Won the third of three starts in Irish bumpers in May, 2010, before joining current connections during the summer. Shaped well on hurdling debut at Newbury in November, finishing 15 lengths second to Kid Cassidy, before overcoming sloppy jumps to beat Herdsman by 13 lengths in extended 2m 4f maiden hurdle at Uttoxeter.

Made all a month later to win a minor event at Leicester by eight lengths before stepping up in class for a Class 2 novices' hurdle over an extended 2m 3f at Ascot, failing by two lengths to concede 3lb to the useful Sonofvic (third 27 lengths away).

Was quietly fancied to run well in Neptune Novices' Hurdle at Cheltenham but was not at his best, struggling to cope with the undulations.

Handled soft ground well but won his bumper in Ireland on firm going, so may be more versatile than last season's form would imply. Was never the best jumper of hurdles but trainer confidently expects him to prove far better over fences.

Stays well and bred to relish three miles. Has a touch of class and could develop into a likely sort for the RSA Chase.

*Tornado Bob – a possible RSA Chase candidate*

## Watch My Back (10yr Bay Gelding)

**Trainer:** Ferdy Murphy
**Pedigree:** Bob Back – Gallants Delight (Idiot's Delight)
**Form:** 0000131P/2010U/0412 -
**Chase Rating:** 150
**Hurdle Rating:** 111
**Optimum Trip:** 2m 4f

Would appear to be fully exposed, having run 22 times, but a very reliable performer when conditions are right and can be relied upon to strike form from his mark in the spring.

Formerly promising with Nicky Richards, winning a bumper and novices' hurdle, before moving to Ferdy Murphy. Has since won four times, proving particularly well suited to flat left-hand tracks, winning handicap chases at Musselburgh (103), Haydock (119), Doncaster (132) and Ayr (137).

Evidence suggests that, despite his age, he is still improving as he is starting the new season from an all-time high mark of 150. Duly took advantage of a fall in the weights last season, winning a 2m 4f Class 2 handicap chase at Ayr in April off 137, having raced off 148 and 142 on his first two starts.

Stepped up on that eight days later, despite not being right, when running Matuhi to a length in a 2m 4f handicap chase at Haydock (145), subsequently raised 5lb to 150 (highest ever mark).

Needs time between his races and expected to be campaigned specifically with spring targets in mind.

# THE DARK HORSES

The following horses are, for the most part, relatively lightly raced and expected to improve significantly this season. The feature includes recruits from Ireland and France.

## Ace High (7yr Bay Gelding)

| | |
|---|---|
| **Trainer:** | Victor Dartnall |
| **Pedigree:** | Kayf Tara – Celtic Native (Be My Native) |
| **Form:** | 0/3022 - |
| **Chase Rating:** | 120 |
| **Hurdle Rating:** | — |
| **Optimum Trip:** | 2m 4f + |

Showed a little promise in a bumper and novice hurdles and ran second in two novice chases last season, at Exeter and Newton Abbot.

Dam comes from an excellent family, a winner herself of 10 of her 16 starts in bumpers, hurdles and chases, out of a half-sister to Grand National winner Red Marauder and Red Striker.

Still a novice for the season and expected to improve for a step up to three miles.

# African Broadway (5yr Bay Gelding)

**Trainer:**        David Pipe
**Pedigree:**       Broadway Flyer – African Lily (Clearly Bust)
**Form:**           1 - 1
**Chase Rating:**   —
**Hurdle Rating:**  —
**Optimum Trip:**   2m 4f +

Shaped well in two Irish point-to-points, falling when in the lead on his debut at Lingstown in April and then running second beaten a neck by Listenlook, later conqueror of Our Father in a novices' hurdle at Chepstow in February.

*Father and son, deep in contemplation*

Came away to win by 16 lengths in the fog on his hurdling debut at Newbury in December then a comfortable winner from Grand Vision in 2m 4f novices' hurdle at Chepstow this October.

Already useful and looks set for a good season in staying novice hurdles and, possibly, novice chases.

## Aland Islands (5yr Bay Gelding)

| | |
|---|---|
| **Trainer:** | Tim Vaughan |
| **Pedigree:** | Stowaway – Champagne Lady (Turtle Island) |
| **Form:** | 1 - |
| **Chase Rating:** | — |
| **Hurdle Rating:** | — |
| **Optimum Trip:** | 2m + |

Imposing chasing type, who had shown enough in work at home to give connections every confidence that he would make a successful racecourse debut when he appeared in a bumper at Exeter in April.

Kept handy most of the way, he went into the lead a quarter of a mile from home and pulled five lengths clear of Russie With Love. Form probably nothing special, but won very comfortably in the manner of a horse who will stay well.

Looks more a galloper than a horse with gears, so likely to start his hurdling career over two and a half miles, perhaps progressing to even further. Promising sort and confidently expected to develop into a decent staying hurdler/chaser.

## All The Aces (6yr Bay Gelding)

| | |
|---|---|
| **Trainer:** | Roger Varian |
| **Pedigree:** | Spartacus – Lili Cup (Fabulous Dancer) |
| **Form:** | — |
| **Chase Rating:** | — |
| **Hurdle Rating:** | — |
| **Optimum Trip:** | 2m + |

Tough and consistent performer on the Flat, currently rated 115, who is expected to be sent hurdling this season (possibly with Nicky Henderson).

Has won just three times, from 15 starts, but has performed regularly in Listed and Group company, notably running well when running second to Kirklees in the 2009 September Stakes at Kempton and winning a Listed contest at Newmarket the previous June.

Has shaped less well in three runs this season, finishing distant third of five to Mahbooba in Listed Godolphin Stakes last time out, but has the class and physique to do well over hurdles. Handles good ground or softer.

Owner Alan Spence is hopeful for this interesting recruit to hurdling.

## Bathwick Brave (4yr Bay Gelding)

| | |
|---|---|
| **Trainer:** | David Pipe |
| **Pedigree:** | Westerner – Dorans Grove (Gildoran) |
| **Form:** | 23 - |
| **Chase Rating:** | — |
| **Hurdle Rating:** | — |
| **Optimum Trip:** | 2m 4f + |

Very green in both starts last season, finishing second and third in bumpers at Taunton and Ffos Las, but displayed a good attitude to keep on well on both occasions.

Did well to figure over two miles, with a dam who won over 2m 4f and who is a daughter of profound influence for stamina Gildoran.

*Westerner – one of the game's most promising sires*

May be vulnerable to anything with gears over two miles but looks the type who will improve in time and over a distance of ground.

## Beat The Rush (4yr Bay Gelding)

**Trainer:** Emma Lavelle
**Pedigree:** Tobougg – Rush Hour (Night Shift)
**Form:** —
**Chase Rating:** —
**Hurdle Rating:** —
**Optimum Trip:** 2m +

Was always well regarded by former handler Julie Camacho but did not progress on the Flat this summer, having won once as a two-year-old (65) and twice last season (75 and 79).

Beaten four times this season (dropped from 85 to 76) but has the ability to make a fair novice hurdler and appeals as the type to pop in at a good price one day. Was prone to race keenly at times, so may be best around sharp tracks.

## Big Occasion (4yr Bay Gelding)

| | |
|---|---|
| **Trainer:** | David Pipe |
| **Pedigree:** | Sadler's Wells – Asnieres (Spend A Buck) |
| **Form:** | — |
| **Chase Rating:** | — |
| **Hurdle Rating:** | — |
| **Optimum Trip:** | 2m 4f + |

Very interesting son of Sadler's Wells, who won twice and finished second twice (blinkered third and fourth starts) from four outings for former handler Aidan O'Brien, winning a 1m 6f handicap in gritty style at the Curragh in October, 2010 (90).

Subsequently joined his new handler and has finished down the field in two 2m 2f handicaps at Newmarket, including the Cesarewitch (95).

Bought with the intention of hurdling and should not be judged on his modest efforts this autumn.

## Bygones Sovereign (5yr Bay Gelding)

| | |
|---|---|
| **Trainer:** | David Pipe |
| **Pedigree:** | Old Vic – Miss Hollygrove (King's Ride) |
| **Form:** | 421 - |
| **Chase Rating:** | — |
| **Hurdle Rating:** | — |
| **Optimum Trip:** | 2m + |

Showed progressive form in bumpers for former handler Karen McLintock, finishing fourth at Sedgefield and second at Ayr before storming clear to beat Victor Hewgo by 17 lengths at Hexham in March.

Half-brother to 2m 4f winner Head Held High out of an unraced sister to useful bumper winner, hurdler and chaser Mister Morose.

Likely to thrive for his new trainer and expected to develop into a useful novice hurdler.

## Captain Conan (4yr Bay Gelding)

**Trainer:** Nicky Henderson
**Pedigree:** Kingsalsa – Lavandou (Sadler's Wells)
**Form:** 341
**Chase Rating:** —
**Hurdle Rating:** —
**Optimum Trip:** 2m +

Unraced on the Flat and has run three times over hurdles since May, winning the Prix Pharaon at Auteuil by 15 lengths on his most recent start.

Described by Anthony Bromley as a "huge youngster", there are hopes that he will show something over hurdles before making his mark over fences next season.

## Close House (4yr Bay Gelding)

**Trainer:** David Pipe
**Pedigree:** Generous – Not Now Nellie (Saddlers' Hall)
**Form:** 212 -
**Chase Rating:** —
**Hurdle Rating:** —
**Optimum Trip:** 2m +

Bought for £100,000 at the Cheltenham Sale in January having finished second and then winning a bumper over 1m 6f at Ayr for Karen McLintock.

No disgrace in finishing second to the very well-regarded Montbazon in a bumper at Doncaster on his first run for these connections in March, with subsequent winners and useful sorts finishing behind.

Dam comes from the family of fair staying chaser Jimmy O'Dea, Morley Street and Granville Again.

Has every chance of becoming one of the best novice hurdlers in his powerful yard. Made quite hard work of winning at Ayr and may need further than two miles to be seen at his best.

## Dannanceys Hill (4yr Bay Gelding)

**Trainer:** Donald McCain
**Pedigree:** Revoque – Some Orchestra (Orchestra)
**Form:** 1
**Chase Rating:** —
**Hurdle Rating:** —
**Optimum Trip:** 2m 4f +

Won his sole start in Irish point-to-points easily, beating Alltheroadrunning by 10 lengths at Kirkistown in the north of Ireland.

Second, third and fifth subsequently beaten but was in great demand at Cheltenham's Brightwells Sales in April before being knocked down to his current trainer for £160,000.

Dam, placed in a 3m hurdle, is a half-sister to the dam of staying chaser Takagi.

Expected to start in a bumper before switching to hurdling. One of the more highly rated young prospects in his yard.

*Donald McCain – has the firepower to have his best ever season*

## Darlan (4yr Brown Gelding)

| | |
|---|---|
| **Trainer:** | Nicky Henderson |
| **Pedigree:** | Milan – Darbela (Doyoun) |
| **Form:** | 1 - |
| **Chase Rating:** | — |
| **Hurdle Rating:** | — |
| **Optimum Trip:** | 2m |

Half-brother to 2m 5f hurdle winner Amie Magnificent out of a mare who won over hurdles and is a half-sister to Prix de Diane and Prix Vermeille winner Daryaba.

Well bred for this game and fully justified market confidence when showing a bright turn of foot to beat Highrate by 27 lengths in a bumper at Haydock in April.

Form upheld this season by fourth, Boruler, who won on his hurdling debut this autumn.

This horse looked in a different class to his rivals and is sure to make a big impact in novice hurdles, perhaps progressing to top company.

## Dildar (3yr Bay Gelding)

| | |
|---|---|
| **Trainer:** | Paul Nicholls |
| **Pedigree:** | Red Ransom – Diamond Tango (Acatenango) |
| **Form:** | — |
| **Chase Rating:** | — |
| **Hurdle Rating:** | — |
| **Optimum Trip:** | 2m |

A smart performer in the spring for the Aga Khan and Alain de Royer-Dupre, winning his second start as a two-year-old and running fourth to subsequent Derby winner Pour Moi in the Group 2 Prix Greffulhe at Saint-Cloud in May, beaten just five and a half lengths. Ran well again next time when second in Listed contest at Bordeaux.

Met with a slight setback after being gelded upon joining this yard but, having been behind the others, is now schooling well and has the class to make an impression in juvenile hurdles. Bred to stay beyond two miles.

## Distant Memories (5yr Bay Gelding)

**Trainer:**          Tom Tate
**Pedigree:**         Falbrav – Amathia (Darshaan)
**Form:**             —
**Chase Rating:**     —
**Hurdle Rating:**    —
**Optimum Trip:**     2m

An interesting recruit to the hurdling ranks, having won six of his 19 starts on the Flat and rated on a mark of 114 at his best.

Has won at Group 3 level and proved especially well suited to soft ground on the Flat. Has looked as good as ever this summer, running well against the likes of Workforce, Await The Dawn and Hunter's Light.

May be significant that connections have decided to give this useful performer a try over hurdles at the age of five. A smooth-traveller on the Flat and should be very hard to beat if he takes to it.

## Dynaste (5yr Grey Gelding)

| | |
|---|---|
| **Trainer:** | David Pipe |
| **Pedigree:** | Martaline – Bellissima De Mai (Pistolet Bleu) |
| **Form:** | 440/3210 - |
| **Chase Rating:** | — |
| **Hurdle Rating:** | 141 |
| **Optimum Trip:** | 2m 4f + |

Shaped well without winning in his three starts in France before running third on his UK debut in a novices' hurdle at Worcester and then second to the very well-treated Aegean Dawn in 2m 5f conditional jockeys' handicap hurdle at Cheltenham (119), failing by three and a half lengths to concede the winner 5lb.

Made all to win extended 2m 3f contest at Taunton in December (130) and then not disgraced on unsuitably good ground in EBF Final at Sandown in March (142).

Handicapper responded harshly to early form with Aegean Dawn but now expected to switch to novice chasing and trainer expects him to relish testing ground.

One to note in novice chases when the mud is flying.

## Eligible (3yr Bay Gelding)

| | |
|---|---|
| **Trainer:** | Tim Vaughan |
| **Pedigree:** | Martaline – Incorrigible (Septieme Ciel) |
| **Form:** | — |
| **Chase Rating:** | — |
| **Hurdle Rating:** | — |
| **Optimum Trip:** | 2m |

Unraced brother to 2m hurdle winner Carabinier out of a well-related unraced mare. Sire doing very well – well-regarded Ozeta, eight-race winner Akarlina and the useful Ayun Tara have won for him.

Bought for 48,000 Euros by Highflyer Bloodstock as a yearling in October, 2009, but never raced and now owned by Dai Walters, so every chance he will make his debut in a bumper at Ffos Las.

*Tim Vaughan, now established as one of our best young trainers*

## Edge Of Town (7yr Bay Gelding)

**Trainer:**        Donald McCain
**Pedigree:**      Witness Box – Hackler Poitin (Little Bighorn)
**Form:**           33/41312/
**Chase Rating:**  —
**Hurdle Rating:**  125
**Optimum Trip:**  3m

Has always been rated a useful prospect for staying chases but had to miss last season after meeting with a setback.

Shaped well when third in both starts in bumpers in January and February, 2009, and the following season won a 2m 6f novices' hurdle on heavy ground at Wetherby and a similar event over an extended 3m at Ayr in February, 2010. Finished second over 3m 1f a month later at Carlisle.

Not expected to scale the heights but clearly stays very well and looks an ideal type for long-distance novice and then handicap chases on heavy ground. Expected to prove a better jumper of fences than he was over hurdles.

## Final Gift (5yr Bay Gelding)

**Trainer:**        Paul Nicholls
**Pedigree:**      Old Vic – Lost Prairie (Be My Native)
**Form:**           21 -
**Chase Rating:**   —
**Hurdle Rating:**  —
**Optimum Trip:**  2m 4f +

One of a handful of Irish point-to-pointers to join this yard, but nominated by the trainer as one who may prove of special interest.

Third foal and the dam an unraced sister to 2m hurdle winner Selous Scout and Beaver Run, from the family of the useful and versatile Young Hustler.

Ran second to Drawn N Drank on debut at Nenagh in January and then ran out a winner by 10 lengths next time at Dromahane.

Expected to prove one of the better staying novice hurdlers in his powerful yard.

*Old Vic, the sire of Final Gift*

## Fingal Bay (5yr Bay Gelding)

**Trainer:** Philip Hobbs
**Pedigree:** King's Theatre – Lady Marguerrite (Blakeney)
**Form:** 1 -
**Chase Rating:** —
**Hurdle Rating:** —
**Optimum Trip:** 2m +

Very hard to assess on the strength of his 22-lengths success in a bumper at Exeter on his sole start. Would possibly have run again at Cheltenham but the ground was deemed too quick and he coughed.

Surprised connections with the margin of his victory as he had not been asked too many questions in his work at home.

Half-brother to staying hurdle and chase winner Oodachee and dam comes from the family of Classic Cliche and My Emma.

Leaves the impression he will stay well.

## Hammersly Lake (3yr Bay Gelding)

**Trainer:**    Nicky Henderson
**Pedigree:**    Kapgarde – Loin De Moi (Loup Solitaire)
**Form:**    31 - 0333
**Chase Rating:**    —
**Hurdle Rating:**    —
**Optimum Trip:**    2m

Quite experienced young hurdler, who has run six times in France in 2011 and rated by noted judge Anthony Bromley as the third-best horse of his generation behind Esmondo and Un Dragon Bleu.

Ran well in all the top races, finishing second to Esmondo on four occasions and getting to within three-quarters of a length of Un Dragon Bleu in the Prix Des Platanes at Auteuil in September.

Will now run in the colours of Michael Buckley in the hope that he develops into a Triumph Hurdle contender. Has the scope to make a chaser in years to come.

# Hinterland (3yr Bay Gelding)

**Trainer:** Paul Nicholls
**Pedigree:** Poliglote – Queen Place (Diamond Prospect)
**Form:** 1
**Chase Rating:** —
**Hurdle Rating:** —
**Optimum Trip:** 2m +

Rated one of the most exciting recruits acquired by Anthony Bromley last season, having won a Listed hurdle race at Auteuil by 10 lengths in May.

Form did not hold up to inspection, with none of the other eight finishers managing to win a race, but the manner of his victory was most impressive and will now run in the colours of Chris Giles and Jared Sullivan, owners of Zarkandar.

May not be seen at his best for a couple of seasons, but rated by all who know him as a horse of great potential.

# Jonny Delta (4yr Chestnut Gelding)

**Trainer:** Jim Goldie
**Pedigree:** Sulamani – Send Me An Angel (Lycius)
**Form:** 10 -
**Chase Rating:** —
**Hurdle Rating:** —
**Optimum Trip:** 2m 4f +

Interesting prospect for hurdling, having won an Ayr bumper very easily by 16 lengths on his racecourse debut last March and then not disgraced when finishing in mid-division in Grade 2 bumper at Aintree.

Was prepared for the Flat, running three times over inadequate trips before qualifying for a mark of 65. Has run reasonably well since then, winning a 1m 5f Class 4 contest at Musselburgh and finishing third twice since (off 71). Now rated 75 on the Flat.

*Jim Goldie – sure to place Jonny Delta with great skill*

A smooth-travelling horse, who is best when held up and ridden off the pace. May be the type to win a novices' handicap hurdle in the spring.

## King's Grace (5yr Bay Gelding)

**Trainer:**       Donald McCain
**Pedigree:**    King's Theatre – Beauchamp Grace (Ardross)
**Form:**          1 -
**Chase Rating:**   —
**Hurdle Rating:**  —
**Optimum Trip:**  2m 4f +

Stoutly-bred half-brother to 2m 5f chase winner Bradford Boris and 2m 4f hurdle winner Beauchamp Gigi out of a mare by strong stamina influence Ardross who stayed three miles.

Made all to win a bumper at Bangor on his sole start in November, surprising the trainer that he was able to win over that trip, but then missed the remainder of the season due to a tumour in his foot.

Confidently expected to develop into a useful staying chaser but can win a race or two over hurdles first. One of the trainer's favourite young horses.

## King's Sunset (6yr Brown Gelding)

**Trainer:**       Tim Vaughan
**Pedigree:**    Old Vic – Dysart Lady (King's Ride)
**Form:**          1 -
**Chase Rating:**   —
**Hurdle Rating:**  —
**Optimum Trip:**  2m 4f +

Left a good impression when winning a point-to-point at Castletown-Geoghegan in April, 2011, benefiting from the fall of odds-on favourite Hereishoping when two lengths clear at the last.

Subsequently acquired for 70,000 Euros at Goffs in May and expected to start in 2m 4f maiden hurdles before stepping up in trip.

Half-brother to David Johnson's useful staying chaser It Takes Time, successful hunter chaser Bright Approach and other winners, out of a mare who won over three miles.

Looks a nice prospect, with the potential to go a long way.

## Kumasi Clan (4yr Bay Gelding)

| | |
|---|---|
| **Trainer:** | Emma Lavelle |
| **Pedigree:** | Moscow Society – Ashanti Dancer (Dancing Dissident) |
| **Form:** | — |
| **Chase Rating:** | — |
| **Hurdle Rating:** | — |
| **Optimum Trip:** | 2m + |

Half-brother to False Economy, a winner on the Flat, over hurdles and over fences for Michael Hourigan. Dam won five races in Holland and is a half-sister to useful Flat and hurdle winner Timber King.

Unraced under any code but has shown loads of talent in work at home and is expected to run well in a bumper before progressing to better things.

## Lets Get Serious (5yr Bay Gelding)

| | |
|---|---|
| **Trainer:** | Nicky Henderson |
| **Pedigree:** | Overbury – Vendimia (Dominion) |
| **Form:** | 1 - |
| **Chase Rating:** | — |
| **Hurdle Rating:** | — |
| **Optimum Trip:** | 2m |

Provided connections with a pleasant surprise when overcoming obvious signs of greenness to beat Dark Lover, a subsequent dual winner, and the promising Sybarite in a Class 4 bumper at Cheltenham in October, 2010. Had not shown much in work at home and showed himself a slow learner in the race, only picking up inside the final quarter mile.

Sire has a reputation for producing quirky sorts, so no surprise to see this half-brother to a 5f winner and a point-to-point winner run in the manner that he did.

Not bred to stay beyond two miles even though he ran as if a distance of ground would suit him.

## Minella Class (6yr Brown Gelding)

**Trainer:** Nicky Henderson
**Pedigree:** Oscar – Louisas Dream (Supreme Leader)
**Form:** 012/1120 -
**Chase Rating:** —
**Hurdle Rating:** 144
**Optimum Trip:** 2m 4f

*Minella Class, hardly 'dark' but a likely top prospect for novice chasing*

Shaped well in Irish point-to-points, notably when running Al Ferof to two lengths at Athlacca on his second start, and went on to beat fair performer Current Resession by a length and a half in a 2m 3f bumper on heavy ground at Naas in February, 2010.

Ran second in another fair bumper next time at Limerick and bought a month later by Anthony Bromley for 95,000gns at the Brightwells Sales in April. Made a good start for his new connections when showing a turn of foot to beat Red Merlin by three and a half lengths on his hurdling debut at Newbury in December. Beat useful Megastar by seven lengths a month later in the Grade 1 Tolworth Hurdle at Sandown before failing to concede 8lb to Aikman in extended 2m 4f Class 2 Sidney Banks Memorial Novices' Hurdle at Huntingdon in February. Ran very well up until the last flight of hurdles when sixth of 12 to First Lieutenant in the Neptune Investment Management Novices' Hurdle at Cheltenham in March.

Best fresh, and thought to have plenty of stamina, but doesn't lack pace and confidently expected to win races over fences. Dam is a half-sister to cross-country performer Heads Onthe Ground, from the family of Marlborough.

Has the class and potential to develop into a high-class novice chaser, initially over two miles and then perhaps over further.

## Mono Man (5yr Bay Gelding)

| | |
|---|---|
| **Trainer:** | Nicky Henderson |
| **Pedigree:** | Old Vic – Quadrennial (Un Desperado) |
| **Form:** | 11 - |
| **Chase Rating:** | — |
| **Hurdle Rating:** | — |
| **Optimum Trip:** | 2m + |

Hard to assess on the evidence of two runs, but trainer rated him one of his best bumper performers last year and there was much to like with the way he went about his business.

Handled the testing ground well when winning a Hereford bumper in January by 17 lengths, pulling well clear from the home turn, and then won a much better contest next time at Ascot, conceding 7lb to Southwell bumper winner Oscara Dara with previous Ascot scorer Persian Snow third.

Connections resisted the temptation to aim at anything better in the spring in the interest of allowing him time to mature and grow into himself.

Bred to stay beyond two miles but doesn't lack pace and expected to make a useful recruit to hurdling.

## Montbazon (4yr Brown Gelding)

**Trainer:**          Alan King
**Pedigree:**         Alberto Giacometti – Duchess Pierji (Cadoudal)
**Form:**             212 -
**Chase Rating:**     —
**Hurdle Rating:**    —
**Optimum Trip:**     2m

Very highly regarded by his trainer but was unfortunate to come up against subsequent Cheltenham Champion Bumper winner Cheltenian on his debut at Kempton.

*Montbazon, probably the pick of Alan King's hurdling recruits*

Made amends next time at Doncaster, staying on well to beat the useful Close House after coming to challenge on the bridle a quarter of a mile from home.

Raised in class for Grade 2 bumper at Aintree but jockey may have been outwitted by the winner Steps To Freedom who, under Paul Carberry, managed to get first run. Pulled eight lengths clear of the third Allure Of Illusion, with some very promising performers stretched out behind.

Has plenty of speed and likely to be kept to two miles for the time being, perhaps taking in another bumper before switching to hurdles. Travels well in his races but showed at Doncaster and Aintree that he can also find plenty when he comes off the bridle.

## Mystic Desir (4yr Chestnut Gelding)

**Trainer:** Jessica Harrington
**Pedigree:** Ballingarry – Aubane (Cadoudal)
**Form:** P3003 - 33
**Chase Rating:** —
**Hurdle Rating:** —
**Optimum Trip:** 2m +

More experienced than many here, having run eight times on the Flat, over hurdles and in handicap chases, showing his best form when third in 4yr old conditions chase at Auteuil in May behind subsequent dual Grade 3 winner Off By Heart.

Third four times, once over hurdles and on last three starts over fences, but has more ability than he has so far shown and is not expected to be a maiden for much longer.

Owned by Michael Buckley and looks an interesting recruit.

## Our Father (5yr Grey Gelding)

| | |
|---|---|
| **Trainer:** | David Pipe |
| **Pedigree:** | Shantou – Rosepan (Taipan) |
| **Form:** | 122 - |
| **Chase Rating:** | — |
| **Hurdle Rating:** | 129 |
| **Optimum Trip:** | 2m 4f + |

Looked set for great things when winning a maiden hurdle on his racecourse debut at Chepstow in January, but proved unable to withstand the challenge of Listenlook over the same course and distance a month later and then again looked one-paced when beaten by Handy Andy in a 2m 5f novices' hurdle at Newbury in March.

Was a weak sort last season and no surprise to see him restricted to just three runs. Dam, runner-up in an Irish point, is a half-sister to staying hurdle and chase winner Caribbean Cove and other fair performers.

Probably being protected for a handicap hurdle before switching to chasing. Left the distinct impression last season that he was a horse of some potential. One to note on his handicap debut, particularly if it is over three miles.

## Ozeta (3yr Grey Filly)

| | |
|---|---|
| **Trainer:** | Nicky Henderson |
| **Pedigree:** | Martaline – Ozehy (Rahy) |
| **Form:** | 1 |
| **Chase Rating:** | — |
| **Hurdle Rating:** | — |
| **Optimum Trip:** | 2m + |

A winner twice on the Flat this summer, taking a 1m 3f Listed contest at Longchamp in May when trained by Elie Lellouche, beating fair performer Avongrove and the subsequent Group 2 and Group 3 winner (also runner-up in Group 1 Prix Vermeille) Testosterone.

Won the Listed Prix Finot on her hurdling debut at Auteuil in September and will now run in the colours of JP McManus.

Qualifies for the fillies' allowance if, as expected, she is raced against the colts and geldings. By a promising sire and has a touch of class.

## Poole Master (6yr Chestnut Gelding)

**Trainer:**      David Pipe
**Pedigree:**     Fleetwood – Juste Belle (Mansonnien)
**Form:**         0/214 -
**Chase Rating:**  —
**Hurdle Rating:**  —
**Optimum Trip:**  2m +

Ran his first race for Chris Down, but joined this yard soon afterwards and failed by just a short head to beat Lucky Landing in a 2m bumper at Uttoxeter in November.

Made amends just 12 days later when beating that winner's stable companion Railway Dillon before running fourth on his hurdling debut to useful performers Minella Class and Red Merlin in an extended 2m maiden hurdle at Newbury.

Seemed to enjoy the soft ground last season and expected to stay well.

## Rich Buddy (5yr Bay Gelding)

**Trainer:**      Richard Phillips
**Pedigree:**     Kayf Tara – Silver Gyre (Silver Hawk)
**Form:**         03 -
**Chase Rating:**  —
**Hurdle Rating:**  —
**Optimum Trip:**  2m 4f +

Half-brother to fair performer Dansilver and 2m 3f hurdle winner Grafite, who shaped better than his finishing position suggests when staying on into third in a bumper

*Richard Phillips, trainer of the promising Rich Buddy*

at Fontwell in March after being almost brought down, losing many lengths and momentum, after half a mile.

Would probably have won at Fontwell had he not been so badly hampered. Bred to stay well and would seem to have more than enough ability to win over hurdles, especially when tried over two and a half miles or more.

## Sam Winner (4yr Bay Gelding)

**Trainer:**       Paul Nicholls
**Pedigree:**      Okawango – Noche (Night Shift)
**Form:**          22/211440 -
**Chase Rating:**  —
**Hurdle Rating:** 145
**Optimum Trip:**  2m 4f

Potentially top-class prospect for novice chasing, having the size and scope to make the switch to fences after showing stacks of ability as a juvenile hurdler.

Shaped well without winning in three starts as a two-year-old in France and then ran second three times over hurdles in fair company at Auteuil. Made an immediate impression on joining this yard, beating the useful Grandouet by 15 lengths at Cheltenham in November and then winning again, by six lengths, over the same course and distance a month later.

Probably found the testing ground against him next time at Chepstow before catching the eye in a major way after struggling with the early pace in the Triumph Hurdle and then powering through up the hill to finish fourth to stable-companion Zarkandar.

Looked likely to be suited to the extra half mile next time at Aintree but dropped away from the third last, possibly over the top for the season.

Has always impressed with his jumping and looks a natural for novice chases, especially in receipt of the four-year-old allowance. Could be anything.

## Storming Gale (5yr Bay Gelding)

**Trainer:**    Donald McCain
**Pedigree:**    Revoque – Dikler Gale (Strong Gale)
**Form:**    1F0 -
**Chase Rating:**    —
**Hurdle Rating:**    —
**Optimum Trip:**    2m 4f +

Won the second of his two starts in Irish point-to-points in March, 2010, by a distance and impressed when winning on his hurdling debut in a 2m 4f maiden contest at Ffos Las last January.

Was held and beaten when falling at the last a month later at Carlisle and weakened half a mile from home on his final outing at Chepstow in April.

Bred for chasing, coming from the family of Newmill and The Dikler. Sure to have benefited from his summer off and expected to prove a fair novice chaser.

## Swincombe Flame (5yr Bay Mare)

| | |
|---|---|
| **Trainer:** | Nick Williams |
| **Pedigree:** | Exit To Nowhere – Lady Felix (Batshoof) |
| **Form:** | 11 - |
| **Chase Rating:** | — |
| **Hurdle Rating:** | — |
| **Optimum Trip:** | 2m |

Impressed when winning a bumper at Warwick on her debut in February, driven clear to win by 11 lengths, and then battled on bravely under a penalty to beat Tante Sissi by two and a quarter lengths in a Listed bumper at Sandown.

Dam won over hurdles at three miles and she needed that stamina when galloping up the hill to win at Sandown.

Looks very promising and will be hard to beat in mares-only races over hurdles.

## Swing Bowler (4yr Bay Filly)

| | |
|---|---|
| **Trainer:** | David Pipe |
| **Pedigree:** | Galileo – Lady Cricket (Cricket Ball) |
| **Form:** | 1 |
| **Chase Rating:** | — |
| **Hurdle Rating:** | — |
| **Optimum Trip:** | 2m |

One of the best-bred mares in training, by world-class sire Galileo out of the very useful hurdler and chaser Lady Cricket.

Won a modest bumper at Wincanton in May very easily by just over three lengths from limited opposition. Expected to compete in another bumper before switching to hurdles. May be aimed at a Listed contest with a view to earning black type for breeding purposes.

## The Pretender (4yr Bay Gelding)

| | |
|---|---|
| **Trainer:** | Paul Nicholls |
| **Pedigree:** | Great Pretender – La Fleur Du Roy (Sleeping Car) |
| **Form:** | 12 |
| **Chase Rating:** | — |
| **Hurdle Rating:** | — |
| **Optimum Trip:** | 2m + |

Won a 1m 7f AQPS bumper in mid-June and then a neck second in a winners' bumper in late July.

Acquired for the Million In Mind partnership and although he is showing sufficient pace for two miles, he will appreciate further in time. Schooling exceptionally well but will start at a modest level before progressing to better things.

## The Weatherman (4yr Bay Gelding)

| | |
|---|---|
| **Trainer:** | Donald McCain |
| **Pedigree:** | Definite Article – Stateable Case (Be My Native) |
| **Form:** | 21 - |
| **Chase Rating:** | — |
| **Hurdle Rating:** | — |
| **Optimum Trip:** | 2m + |

Half-brother to the same stable's useful mare Dorabelle out of a full sister to Colonel Yeager and 3m chase winner Amelia Earhart.

Confirmed the promise shown when second in a bumper last May at Kelso when returning to the track to win a bumper by 10 lengths, leading a quarter of a mile from home and staying on strongly in the closing stages.

Trainer rates him quite highly and he has every chance of developing into a useful novice hurdler.

## Tornade D'Estruval (4yr Bay Filly)

**Trainer:** Nicky Henderson
**Pedigree:** Network – Onde D'Estruval (Art Bleu)
**Form:** 001 -
**Chase Rating:** —
**Hurdle Rating:** —
**Optimum Trip:** 2m

By the same sire as Sprinter Sacre and won a minor event at Vichy in May very easily for Guillaume Macaire before joining this trainer for Million In Mind.

Has shown plenty of ability in her work and schooling over fences, and expected to alternate between hurdling and chasing, possibly at Listed level.

## Turanjo Bello (4yr Grey Gelding)

**Trainer:** Philip Hobbs
**Pedigree:** Turgeon – Tchi Tchi Bang Bang (Perrault)
**Form:** 2 -
**Chase Rating:** —
**Hurdle Rating:** —
**Optimum Trip:** 2m 4f +

Not an obvious inclusion from such a powerful yard, but comes here highly recommended by the trainer and looks sure to improve on his promising second in the first division of a 3m point-to-point at Templemore last April.

Winner, Flying Vic, now with Tim Vaughan, and fourth Whats Happening won next time out.

Has shown enough at home to warrant a run in a bumper and bought by Diana and Grahame Whateley, owners of Captain Chris and Wishfull Thinking.

# Volcan Surprise (3yr Bay Gelding)

**Trainer:** Alan King
**Pedigree:** Dom Alco – Invitee Surprise (April Night)
**Form:** 42
**Chase Rating:** —
**Hurdle Rating:** —
**Optimum Trip:** 2m +

By the sire of Grands Crus, Al Ferof and Neptune Collonges and shaped with great promise in his two starts over hurdles at Clairefontaine in July, finishing fourth and then second.

Has been schooling very well this autumn and expected to take high rank as a juvenile hurdler.

# THE HANDICAP PROJECTS

The following horses have left the impression that they have been campaigned with handicaps in mind. You are advised to monitor the market carefully when they appear.

## Agapanthus (6yr Bay Gelding)

| | |
|---|---|
| **Trainer:** | Barney Curley |
| **Pedigree:** | Tiger Hill – Astilbe (Monsun) |
| **Form:** | 0/000 - 0 |
| **Chase Rating:** | — |
| **Hurdle Rating:** | 89 |
| **Optimum Trip:** | 2m |

*Barney Curley – always one step ahead of the game*

Has won four times on the Flat, as part of the stable's big coup at Brighton off 63 in May, 2010, and then again next time from a mark of 71 at Sandown.

Has not won since, and has shown precious little in five runs over hurdles in being beaten 101 lengths, 64 lengths, pulled up, 63 lengths and 31 lengths.

Trainer prepared to wait as long as required for the right opportunity to come along, so watch the market carefully when this one next appears over hurdles. Horses from the yard generally run best after a lengthy break.

## Castlerock (7yr old Grey Gelding)

**Trainer:**       Jonjo O'Neill
**Pedigree:**      Kayf Tara – Jessolle (Scallywag)
**Form:**          302/00 - 2
**Chase Rating:**  —
**Hurdle Rating:** 115
**Optimum Trip:**  3m +

Half-brother to Bakbenscher and could hardly be more stoutly bred, from the family of Better Times Ahead out of a mare by Scallywag.

Shaped quite well in a bumper and two novice hurdles in 2009/10 but lightly raced last season, finishing down the field in his first two races before returning from a break to finish second to Red Not Blue in an extended 2m 4f 0-115 handicap hurdle at Southwell in June.

Has not been without his problems, but could be one to keep in mind for a long-distance staying novices' handicap chase.

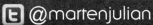

## De Boitron (7yr Bay Gelding)

**Trainer:** Ferdy Murphy
**Pedigree:** Sassanian – Pondiki (Sicyos)
**Form:** 000121/0243 -
**Chase Rating:** 137
**Hurdle Rating:** —
**Optimum Trip:** 2m 4f

Been around a while, having run 30 times since making his debut in France five years ago, but still seemed to be improving last season notably when finishing fourth in the Grand Annual Chase at Cheltenham (137) and then third to Poquelin in Grade 2 limited handicap over 2m 5f at the same course in April (13lb out of the handicap).

Seems at his most effective on good ground, winning at Doncaster and Cheltenham last spring from marks of 120 and 126. Put up some fair efforts thereafter, without winning, rising to his current mark.

Has the ability to win a decent handicap chase, either this autumn or on the good ground in the spring.

## Desert Cry (5yr Brown Gelding)

**Trainer:** Donald McCain
**Pedigree:** Desert Prince – Hataana (Robellino)
**Form:** 02120 -
**Chase Rating:** —
**Hurdle Rating:** 135
**Optimum Trip:** 2m

Fair performer on the Flat in France, winning five, second five and third four times from 23 starts at a reasonable level.

Keen on his debut over hurdles at Leicester in January, but then ran fair second to useful Darna at Ayr before winning on the bridle in modest company at Sedgefield. Stepped up in grade for Grade 2 novices' event at Kelso over 2m 2f but didn't stay the trip in the soft ground. Again disappointing next time at Aintree, racing keenly again and not coming home.

Needs to settle better and may be suited to running in a more competitive race. Handles soft ground but struggles to get a yard beyond two miles.

Likely to be aimed at a decent handicap hurdle but may be switched to chasing if schooling goes well.

---

## First Fandango (4yr Bay Gelding)

| | |
|---|---|
| **Trainer:** | Tim Vaughan |
| **Pedigree:** | Hernando – First Fantasy (Be My Chief) |
| **Form:** | 110 - 3 |
| **Chase Rating:** | — |
| **Hurdle Rating:** | 134 |
| **Optimum Trip:** | 2m |

Fair performer on the Flat for John Hills, winning just once (73) but running consistently on most other occasions, finishing second or third on seven of his 11 other starts.

Equipped with a tongue-tie on all his five outings since joining this yard after being bought for 60,000gns at Brightwells in October, 2010 (bought again by this trainer for 18,000gns at Doncaster in April, 2011). Made a successful hurdling debut at Ffos Las last November and then battled on bravely to beat the useful Vosges by a head at Ayr in January.

Next appeared in the Triumph Hurdle where, visored for the first time, he was beaten 26 lengths before running on the Flat at Wolverhampton in April. Hampered on his return to action at Cheltenham in October and likely to be prepared for a decent handicap hurdle in the spring.

May have a few pounds in hand of this mark.

## Going Wrong (8yr Bay Gelding)

**Trainer:** Ferdy Murphy
**Pedigree:** Bob Back – Lucy Glitters (Ardross)
**Form:** 0/440/12/
**Chase Rating:** —
**Hurdle Rating:** 130
**Optimum Trip:** 2m 4f +

Very interesting lightly-raced prospect, having run just six times in three seasons. Dam won at three miles and is from the family of top chaser Dublin Flyer.

Shaped well when staying on from arrears in bumpers at Haydock and Newcastle (2008). Again indicated that he required a test of stamina when distant fourth on hurdling debut in November, 2008, but then looked slow when beaten 20 lengths in 3m 2f novices' hurdle at Huntingdon a month later.

Given time off and returned in a 2m 4f novices' hurdle at Carlisle in November, 2009, making all and staying on gamely to beat the useful Wymott by two lengths (third 20 lengths away). Raced too keenly next time at Newcastle but still ran well, failing by a neck to concede 5lb to Bygones Of Brid after being hampered at the second last, with useful Diklers Oscar and Heez A Steel back in third and fourth.

Subsequently got cast in his box and broke a pelvis when at livery but has been back in his yard since the summer and has impressed in his schooling over fences at home.

Bred to stay well but does not lack pace and expected to prove a very effective novice chaser. Rated highly by his trainer.

## Hildisvini (5yr Bay Gelding)

| | |
|---|---|
| **Trainer:** | Charlie Longsdon |
| **Pedigree:** | Milan – Site Mistress (Remainder Man) |
| **Form:** | 02111 - |
| **Chase Rating:** | — |
| **Hurdle Rating:** | 135 |
| **Optimum Trip:** | 2m 4f |

Ran sixth and second in two bumper starts for his former handler before making a winning debut for his new connections at Warwick in January, responding bravely to strong driving from the turn out of the back straight.

Beat the highly-rated Kid Cassidy on his hurdling debut in similar style next time at Sandown, finding more than the winner between the last two, before beating Cleaver by half a length in 2m 4f novices' hurdle at Lingfield.

Half-brother to 3m hurdle and chase winner Nostringsattached out of a half-sister to the very useful staying chaser Streamstown.

Displayed a gritty attitude last season and is particularly well suited to testing conditions and a distance of ground. Sure to benefit from three miles and has an exciting future as a staying chaser. May be aimed at a valuable long-distance handicap hurdle before then. Very tough.

## Highland Valley (6yr Chestnut Gelding)

| | |
|---|---|
| **Trainer:** | Emma Lavelle |
| **Pedigree:** | Flemensfirth – Loch Lomond (Dry Dock) |
| **Form:** | 1/1410 - |
| **Chase Rating:** | — |
| **Hurdle Rating:** | 134 |
| **Optimum Trip:** | 2m 4f + |

Made a successful racecourse debut in a bumper at Wincanton in February, 2010 and most impressive to the eye when winning on his hurdling debut at Exeter the following November, challenging on the bridle and quickening away from the last to win without coming under pressure.

Ran very well, despite a number of sloppy jumps, next time out when fourth to Mossley in the 3m Grade 2 Albert Bartlett (Bristol) Novices' Hurdle. Returned to winning form two months later when beating the consistent Araldur by two lengths at Exeter, battling on very gamely after the last to concede the runner-up 7lb.

Not disgraced when running well until the second last on his final outing in the Grade 1 Neptune Novices' Hurdle at Cheltenham.

May stay over hurdles for the time being to try and exploit what his trainer believes may be a favourable mark. A decision will then be made regarding a possible switch to fences.

## Hold On Julio (8yr Brown Gelding)

**Trainer:** Alan King
**Pedigree:** Blueprint – Eileens Native (Be My Native)
**Form:** PP/1 -
**Chase Rating:** 117
**Hurdle Rating:** —
**Optimum Trip:** 2m 4f +

Formerly owned and trained by Vicky Simpson and the winner of four point-to-points in the north of England, this son of Blueprint showed a sparkling turn of foot to win a maiden hunters' chase at Kelso in April with any amount in hand. Bought by his new connections at the Doncaster sales for £28,000.

Formerly affected by stomach ulcers (pulled up as a younger horse in novice hurdles), he looks extremely well treated on a mark of 117 for his new handler.

Dam, unraced, comes from the family of Go Native, Indian Solitaire and Hopscotch. Stays three miles well but does not lack speed and may well prove effective over shorter trips. Very interesting.

## Horatio Caine (4yr Bay Gelding)

| | |
|---|---|
| **Trainer:** | Nick Williams |
| **Pedigree:** | Assessor – Red Flower (Trempolino) |
| **Form:** | 0400 - |
| **Chase Rating:** | — |
| **Hurdle Rating:** | 119 |
| **Optimum Trip:** | 2m 4f + |

Showed promise on sole start over hurdles in France last September (2010) and highly tried in both outings here last season, finishing behind Sam Winner at Cheltenham in November and December.

Went back to France for another run in March, finishing tailed off, but now rated on a mark of 119 and may improve for the step into handicaps.

Bred to stay well, so may pay to watch in long-distance novice handicap hurdles. Almost certainly capable of better than he has shown.

## Ibn Hiyyan (4yr Grey Gelding)

| | |
|---|---|
| **Trainer:** | Ferdy Murphy |
| **Pedigree:** | El Prado – Lovely Later (Green Dancer) |
| **Form:** | 0004 - |
| **Chase Rating:** | — |
| **Hurdle Rating:** | 96 |
| **Optimum Trip:** | 2m + |

Nominated by the trainer as a horse to watch last season but failed to show much in four starts over hurdles, beaten an aggregate of 139 lengths.

Especially disappointing at Southwell in April, weakening from the third last and beaten 30 lengths. Dropped 3lb, from 99 to 96.

Showed ability with Mark Johnston on the Flat, making all to win a modest 1m 4f 0-60 race at Southwell in April, 2010.

Has been schooled over fences and may run in a novices' handicap chase rather than stick to hurdles. Capable of better than he has so far shown and has every chance of moving forwards from his mark.

---

## Makhzoon (7yr Bay Gelding)

| | |
|---|---|
| **Trainer:** | Tim Vaughan |
| **Pedigree:** | Dynaformer – Boubskaia (Niniski) |
| **Form:** | 303/0310/0 - 121 |
| **Chase Rating:** | — |
| **Hurdle Rating:** | 122 |
| **Optimum Trip:** | 3m |

Consistent and progressive former 240,000 Euros yearling purchase, who never ran on the Flat but shaped well in bumpers and over hurdles for Paul Webber before winning 2m conditional jockeys' event on heavy ground at Leicester on his first start for this trainer in December, 2009.

Returned to winning form last April, landing an extended 2m 7f handicap hurdle at Fakenham (109) and then second, beaten a nose, in a similar 3m race at Ludlow (115) before staying on strongly to beat Rolecarr by a neck at Wetherby in June (117).

Has done well to win on good ground because his trainer believes he is better suited to more testing conditions. Almost definitely has something more in hand and could be the right type for the Pertemps series.

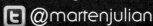

## Night In Milan (5yr Bay Gelding)

**Trainer:**     Keith Reveley
**Pedigree:**     Milan – Chione (Mandalus)
**Form:**     0/00013100 -
**Chase Rating:**     —
**Hurdle Rating:**     107
**Optimum Trip:**     2m 4f +

Very stoutly-bred son of Milan out of an Irish point-winning relation to top-class staying hurdler Rose Ravine.

Ran in a bumper at Perth and then three educational runs over hurdles before winning an extended 2m 4f 0-90 handicap hurdle at Southwell by half a length from I Can Run Can You (off 90). Stayed on to finish third a week later under a 7lb penalty in a 2m 4f handicap hurdle at Sedgefield before winning a 2m 4f 0-100 handicap hurdle on heavy ground at Newcastle (100).

Ill-suited by the drop back to two miles next time (112) and disappointing on his final start in a 3m 0-130 handicap hurdle at Newcastle (110).

Subsequently dropped to 107 and should improve sufficiently to capitalise on that mark. Bred to stay long distances and may be one to note for a staying novices' chase when the mud is flying. Has probably been brought along steadily with the long-term in mind.

## Railway Dillon (6yr Bay Gelding)

**Trainer:**     Donald McCain
**Pedigree:**     Witness Box – Laura's Native (Be My Native)
**Form:**     22312 -
**Chase Rating:**     —
**Hurdle Rating:**     125
**Optimum Trip:**     2m 4f +

The ground cannot be soft enough for this stoutly-bred son of Witness Box. Won the third of three starts in Irish point-to-points and finished second on his UK debut for these connections in a 2m bumper at Uttoxeter in November.

Stepped up to extended 2m 4f for his hurdling debut at the same track a month later and finished second again, then third to Minella Stars over extended 2m 6f at Hereford before staying on very dourly to beat Fourjacks by a diminishing half length in a 2m 4f novices' hurdle at Newcastle in February.

Ran well later in the month when second to Our Island in extended 3m novices' hurdle at Newbury, keeping on very gamely indeed under pressure.

Lacks gears but impressed enormously with his attitude last season and looks the perfect type for staying novice handicap chases, especially when conditions are testing.

---

## Rollwiththepunches (6yr Bay Gelding)

**Trainer:**        Ferdy Murphy
**Pedigree:**      Hernando – Zarma (Machiavellian)
**Form:**           330/3120/030 –
**Chase Rating:**  —
**Hurdle Rating:** 128
**Optimum Trip:**  2m +

Always showed ability at home for former trainer Charlie McBride and hinted at his potential when running second to Captain Chris in a novices' hurdle at Kempton in March, 2010.

Failed to progress from there last season, running best from three runs when third to Shoegazer off 130 in a 2m 4f 0-145 handicap hurdle at Ffos Las in February, 2011.

Made all on the sole occasion he was successful – at Huntingdon in January, 2010 – and has been schooling over fences since arriving in this yard.

Not an obvious one for inclusion but connections are quietly hopeful there is better to come and the change of scenery may encourage him to fulfil his potential.

## Savaronola (6yr Chestnut Gelding)

| | |
|---|---|
| **Trainer:** | Barney Curley |
| **Pedigree:** | Pulpit – Running Debate (Open Forum) |
| **Form:** | 00/00/3 - |
| **Chase Rating:** | — |
| **Hurdle Rating:** | 75 |
| **Optimum Trip:** | 2m |

Has won just once from 20 lifetime starts on the Flat and over jumps, playing an important part in a well-organised stable coup when landing a modest 1m 4f 0-55 handicap by six lengths at Wolverhampton in May, 2010.

Has run five times over hurdles, beaten 95 lengths and 51 lengths on his third and fourth starts in 2009/10 having been beaten 154 lengths on his hurdling debut for former connections at Roscommon in August, 2008 and again next time at Killarney.

Showed a little promise when third on handicap hurdle debut at Market Rasen in June, 2010 (75).

Not been seen out since over hurdles, but has been shaping reasonably well on the Flat and would be nicely poised to win a handicap hurdle or two from his current lowly mark. As always with this yard market movements will prove informative.

## Seigneur Des Bois (5yr Bay Gelding)

| | |
|---|---|
| **Trainer:** | Ferdy Murphy |
| **Pedigree:** | Ballingarry – Studieuse (Snurge) |
| **Form:** | 3P041340/3000021 - |
| **Chase Rating:** | 111 |
| **Hurdle Rating:** | — |
| **Optimum Trip:** | 2m |

Has raced at a modest level so far but seemed to be improving last spring and has the scope to progress again.

Ran consistently over hurdles and fences in France but didn't show much in his early outings in the UK, beaten a long way in novice chase company at Carlisle (three times) and Sedgefield. Ran better when second off 103 in a handicap chase at Bangor before beating Haka Dancer in a 2m 0-110 novices' handicap chase at Southwell, appearing to struggle early on before staying on strongly in the closing stages.

Still favourably treated on the evidence of his French form and looks just the type his trainer places so well to win in the spring.

## Seven Summits (4yr Bay Gelding)

**Trainer:**      Barney Curley
**Pedigree:**    Danehill Dancer – Mandavilla (Sadler's Wells)
**Form:**         000 -
**Chase Rating:**  —
**Hurdle Rating:**  106
**Optimum Trip:**  2m

Won an extended 1m 2f maiden at Dundalk for Aidan O'Brien in July, 2010, and then ran in handicaps at Ascot and Doncaster for Jeremy Noseda before joining this yard after being bought for 40,000gns from Tattersalls in October, 2010.

Given three runs over hurdles in the spring of last year, two in February and one in April, and has since run twice on the Flat at Newmarket (off 90 and 82).

Has not yet given his new trainer a return from his investment but has shown enough to suggest he will do so when conditions come right. Hard to assess on the limited evidence to date, but stayed on from arrears on third start at Stratford in April and looks an interesting prospect for when the right race comes along.

# Tenor Nivernais (4yr Bay Gelding)

| | |
|---|---|
| **Trainer:** | Venetia Williams |
| **Pedigree:** | Shaanmer – Hosanna II (Marasail) |
| **Form:** | 11330 - |
| **Chase Rating:** | — |
| **Hurdle Rating:** | 124 |
| **Optimum Trip:** | 2m 4f + |

Won twice over hurdles in the French Provinces in August, 2010, and made UK debut when third in 2m 0-120 handicap hurdle at Wincanton in January (118).

Filled same position the following month at Taunton (119) before catching the eye with a strong finish from off the pace after being hampered in the Fred Winter Juvenile Handicap Hurdle at Cheltenham (124).

Looked quite eye-catching at Cheltenham, staying on in a manner suggesting he would appreciate a step up in trip.

Trainer adept at placing horses of this type and looks a likely sort for a big prize, possibly in one of the season's more valuable handicaps.

# TRAINERS' SELECTIONS

Ladbrokes have kindly agreed to cover the profit made to level stakes for every selection in this feature at £2 a point. For example, this means that if a nominated horse wins at 5/1 and then loses twice, the horse has made a profit to level stakes of 5 points, less 2, which is 3 points. That horse has therefore earned £6 (3 x £2). The total sum from the LSP on all the horses will be donated by Ladbrokes to the Injured Jockeys' Fund.

## Kim Bailey
### Mallusk (6yr Bay Gelding)
*(Exit To Nowhere – Saucy Nun)*
*Trainer says:* "Still on the right side of the handicapper."

## Tony Carroll
### Walden Prince (4yr Bay Gelding)
*(Saffron Walden – Kahyasi Princess)*
*Trainer says:* "He has recently been purchased from Denis Cullen in Ireland. He goes for a novices' handicap hurdle at the Paddy Power meeting at Cheltenham on 12 November. Zafranagar won the corresponding race for the yard in 2009. Walden Prince moves very well at home."

## Noel Chance
### Gores Island (5yr Bay Gelding)
*(Beneficial – Just Leader)*
*Marten says:* "Shaped well in two bumpers at Southwell and Fontwell last season. Sure to do well when put over hurdles, perhaps over further than two miles."

## Henry Daly
### Grove Pride (6yr Bay Gelding)
*(Double Trigger – Dara's Pride)*

*Marten says:* "Shaped well when second and third in two bumpers last season. From the family of Our Ben and bred to stay long distances."

## Victor Dartnall
### Connak (9yr Chestnut Gelding)
*(Pasternak – Call Me Connie)*
*Trainer says:* "Classy ex-Robert Alner novice chaser who has dropped to a reasonable mark of 125 after a break."

## James Ewart
### Conceptual Art (4yr Bay Colt)
*(Haafhd – Hasty Words)*
*Marten says:* "Showed some ability without winning in three runs on the Flat for Michael Bell."

## Tom George
### Module (4yr Bay Colt)
*(Panoramic – Before Royale)*
*Trainer says:* "Winner of a four-year-old hurdle in France."

## Chris Grant
### Brokethegate (6yr Bay Gelding)
*(Presenting – Briery Ann)*
*Marten says:* "Showed a modicum of promise in two bumpers and then beaten a long way on his hurdling debut at Kelso. May do better over a longer trip."

## Micky Hammond
### Franks A Million (4yr Bay Gelding)
*(Blueprint – Ballys Baby)*
*Marten says:* "Unraced four-year-old by Blueprint from the family of Merry Master and Back On Line."

## Jessica Harrington
### The Engineer (5yr Bay Gelding)
(Old Vic – Mother Superior)

*Trainer says:* "The Engineer was placed in two good bumpers last year has the makings of a chaser in time."

*and*

### Beachdale Lad (4yr Chestnut Gelding)
(Carroll House – Morning Clare)

*Trainer says:* "Beachdale Lad won a point to point last spring looks a nice horse."

## Nicky Henderson
### Heather Royal (5yr Chestnut Mare)
(Medicean – Close Harmony)

*Trainer says:* "As a half-sister to Barbers Shop she jumps well and should win hurdle races."

## Philip Hobbs
### Turanjo Bello (4yr Grey Gelding)
(Turgeon – Tchi Tchi Bang Bang)

*Trainer says:* "Second in his only Irish point-to-point. Will run him in bumpers in December."

## Michael Hourigan
### Clear Hills (4yr Bay Gelding)
(Marju – Rainbows For All)

*Trainer says:* "I think Clear Hills is one to look out for. He has won a point to point and will head for a bumper shortly.

*and*

### Ballysteen (5yr Bay Gelding)
(Elnadim – Winning Jenny)

*Trainer says:* "Ballysteen is a nice horse who I hope can do very well."

## Alan King
### Hold On Julio (8yr Brown Gelding)
(Blueprint – Eileens Native)

Trainer says: "Northern point-to-point and hunter chase winner. Showing plenty of ability and is interesting off mark of 116."

## Neil King
### Good Faloue (6yr Bay Mare)
(Kahyasi – Good Blend)

Marten says: "Has been around a bit, winning once from 13 starts, but has dropped to a mark of 95 over hurdles from 107 and may be capable of winning before switching to fences."

## Henrietta Knight
### Loch Ba (5yr Bay Gelding)
(Craigsteel – Lenmore Lisa)

Trainer says: "Always a chaser in the making. A lovely type and plenty of ability."

## Emma Lavelle
### Penny Max (5yr Bay Gelding)
(Flemensfirth – Ballymartin Trix)

Trainer says: "Progressive likes soft ground and could be exciting."

## Richard Lee
### Black Is Beautiful (3yr Bay Gelding)
(Black Sam Bellamy – Queen's Theatre)

Trainer says: "Unraced three-year-old son of Black Sam Bellamy, who will run in three-year-old bumpers."

## Gary Moore
### Bert The Alert (3yr Bay Gelding)
(Proclamation – Megalex)

Trainer says: "Nice horse who goes well and is well-related."

## Willie Mullins
### Raptor (6yr Grey Gelding)
*(Caballo Raptor – Tiwa)*

*Marten says:* "Ex-French and won a maiden 2m 4f maiden hurdle at Punchestown and not disgraced in Grade 2 contest in May."

## Ferdy Murphy
### Sendiym (4yr Bay Colt)
*(Rainbow Quest – Seraya)*

*Trainer says:* "Sharp four-year-old, who jumps well."

## Paul Nicholls
### Final Gift (5yr Bay Gelding)
*(Old Vic – Lost Prairie)*

*Trainer says:* "Very promising young point-to-point winner."

## Paul Nolan
### King Vuvuzela (4yr Bay Gelding)
*(Flemensfirth – Coolgavney Girl)*

*Marten says:* "Won a Punchestown bumper in May and then fair fifth in maiden hurdle at Cork."

## Edward O'Grady
### Do Brazil (5yr Chestnut Gelding)
*(Flemensfirth – Ballybeg Rose)*

*Trainer says:* "Showed good promise in bumpers last season. Should make a nice novice hurdler."

## Richard Phillips
### Rich Buddy (5yr Bay Gelding)
*(Kayf Tara – Silver Gyre)*

*Marten says:* "Very stoutly bred, so did well to show ability in two bumpers. Likely to relish a test of stamina."

## David Pipe
### Bygones Sovereign (5yr Bay Gelding)
*(Old Vic – Miss Hollygrove)*

*Trainer says:* "Hopefully will make a nice staying hurdler."

## Brendan Powell
### Bennys Well (5yr Bay Gelding)
*(Beneficial – Alure)*

*Trainer says:* "Finished second in a decent bumper at Towcester and jumps well. Should be out very shortly."

## John Queally
### Memories Of Milan (5yr Bay Gelding)
*(Milan – Be My Rainbow)*

*Marten says:* "Won a 2m 4f maiden hurdle and placed twice. Related to stayers and should do well in novice chases."

## John Quinn
### Moonlight Drive (5yr Bay Gelding)
*(Oscar – Perspex Queen)*

*Trainer says:* "Will go straight novice chasing. Should not have run at Cheltenham as the ground was too quick. A fine, quality horse, who will do well. Ready to run in November."

## Philip Rothwell
### Dont Tell The Boys (5yr Grey Gelding)
*(Silver Patriarch – Deep C Diva)*

*Trainer says:* "We feel he will win a race or two over the coming months and would be worth following as our horses are back to form. He will go chasing shortly."

## Oliver Sherwood
### Florafern (6yr Bay Mare)
*(Alflora – Mossy Fern)*
*Trainer says:* "Very unlucky in three bumpers. A must in mare novice hurdles!"

## Tom Tate
### Distant Memories (5yr Bay Gelding)
*(Falbrav – Amathia)*
*Marten says:* "Very useful performer on the Flat, rated 114 at his best, and well suited to soft ground. Will make an interesting recruit to the hurdling scene."

## Tim Vaughan
### Jimbil (5yrBrown Gelding)
*(Flying Legend – Ah Gowan)*
*Trainer says:* "Winner of both his starts, look open to lots of progression and best on good ground."

## Tim Walford
### Fentara (6yr Bay Mare)
*(Kayf Tara – Miss Fencote)*
*Trainer says:* "May improve over fences."

## Dermot Weld
### Galileo's Choice (5yr Bay Gelding)
*(Galileo – Sevi's Choice)*
*Trainer says:* "Hardly a dark horse but should make into a very decent novice hurdler. He does not like really winter ground."

# Be free with Ladbrokes Mobile

**Bet After The Off**     **Best Odds Guaranteed***

**Live Results**     **Free Download**

**GOT THE FEELIN**
GET TO
*Ladbrokes*

Go to **mobile.ladbrokes.com**
or text **MOBILE** to **86131**

# THE 2012 CHELTENHAM GOLD CUP PREVIEW

**Long Run**, the winner of 12 of his 18 starts and second or third in the other six, is a thoroughly worthy favourite for the 2012 Gold Cup even though a top price of 5/2 may not appeal to long-range backers.

However it is not hard to understand why the bookmakers are reluctant to offer anything more generous.

In winning the 2011 Gold Cup by seven lengths, Long Run beat the winners of the last four runnings together with others that had run well in the race before. They were joined by Irish Hennessy winner Kempes and Lexus Chase winner Pandorama

*Long Run – at his exuberant best*

and, in winning, Long Run became the first six-year-old to land the Gold Cup since the great Mill House back in 1963. Also, Sam Waley-Cohen became the first amateur to ride the Gold Cup winner since Jim Wilson on Little Owl in 1981. The race was run in a track-record time, although the trip was reported to be 80 yards shorter than in previous years.

The big doubt about Long Run approaching the Festival was his jumping. Indeed, some would argue that this remains a concern.

He had made a succession of mistakes on his previous two visits to Cheltenham, also looking ill-suited to the track, having jumped appallingly on his first two starts in the UK at Kempton, on Boxing Day, 2009, and then at Warwick.

Although his fencing technique had improved by the time the Gold Cup came along, it was still not without blemish, getting close to the third, tenth, twelfth, fourth-last and third-last fences. Having said that he never looked like falling, even if at times he lost momentum, and it surprised me that he had sufficient reserves to power away from Denman and Kauto Star on the run to the last.

There was a point turning for home where Long Run seemed to be travelling less well than either Denman or Kauto Star – something reflected in his in-running price of 11 on Betfair – which is why that surge approaching the last and up the run to the line was so impressive. Here was evidence that this young horse not only possessed great talent, but also courage and tenacity in equal measure. Earplugs, which had been applied for the first time in the King George, may have helped.

There was talk of Long Run trying to emulate Mandarin's feat in 1962 by trying to follow up his Gold Cup triumph with a crack at the Grand Steeple-Chase de Paris but, as he had lost 15 kilos in the race, connections decided to put the plan on hold. There were also issues relating to Sam Waley-Cohen's eligibility to ride.

Owner Robert Waley-Cohen, the new chairman of Cheltenham Racecourse, has ambitious plans for Long Run. He would like his horse to attain a higher BHA figure than Kauto Star, who was rated on 193 after landing the King George VI Chase at Kempton in December, 2009. Long Run was raised 3lb, from 179 to 182, after Cheltenham so he has another 11lb to find.

Waley-Cohen said in the autumn:

"There is no point in being modest about this. I'd like people to say 'that's the best horse I've ever seen in my life'. Best Mate won three Gold Cups but actually his top

*The magnificent Kauto Star*

rating was never very impressive. We only think of what Arkle did and I think he was rated 212. That is an acknowledgement of where you stand against other horses in history."

Trainer Nicky Henderson expressed his delight with Long Run's condition when speaking in the autumn, stating that the horse had "grown and filled out". His season will start with a clash against Kauto Star in Haydock's Betfair Chase in November before the King George, while he added that Liverpool may also be a consideration after Cheltenham now that there is a four-week gap between the two meetings.

Long Run is now established as the best staying chaser in training and, at the age of six, it is reasonable to expect further improvement to come from him. The chief concern is his jumping which, though much improved, remains flawed. Yet he is nimble on his feet and, in 10 starts over fences, has never fallen.

I would not, though, wish to commit to an ante-post bet at 5/2 at this early stage while that risk remains.

The future for **Kauto Star** is uncertain. Paul Nicholls put out a positive message about the horse in September, confirming the intention to tackle Long Run in the

Betfair Chase at Haydock on 19 November – a race he won in 2006, 2007 and 2009.

The dual Gold Cup winner, and four-time King George VI Chase winner, was pulled up in the Punchestown Guinness Gold Cup on his final appearance last season. However he returned to training in August and is reported by his handler to be "in great order". Nicholls now concedes that the horse should never have gone to Ireland and that a decision on his future will be made after he runs at Haydock.

Last season Kauto Star twice finished behind Long Run, beaten 19 lengths at Kempton and then 11 lengths in the Gold Cup. He will be 12 next March, and you have to go back to What A Myth in 1969 to find the last horse of that age to win the race.

Kauto Star was probably at his best when he trounced Madison Du Berlais – a horse then rated on 169 - by 36 lengths in the fourth of his King George triumphs

The evidence from last year, as reflected in his 23lb lower rating, is that he is no longer the horse he was. My view is that Kauto Star will be retired before the spring, a rest richly deserved after the pleasure he has given since first impressing me on his UK debut at Newbury back in December, 2004.

There are just two targets for **Denman** this season – the Lexus Chase at Leopardstown and a fifth appearance in the Gold Cup, a race in which he has finished first or second in the last four runnings.

Denman has finished in the first three in all but two of his 22 completed outings – he fell and unseated on two occasions – with his two unplaced efforts coming when he was asked to race in the month following his Gold Cup efforts.

Like Kauto Star, Denman will be 12 in March and history is against him landing the race for a second time. However, given his exceptional record in the race, Denman has claims to being rated the second-best staying chaser in training and if anything were to happen to Long Run he could be the one to benefit the most.

He had Kauto Star and What A Friend four lengths and a nose behind him in last year's Gold Cup and I would not discourage anyone from a speculative interest at 25/1, a price which the horse's loyal fans will consider derisory. The intention to aim him at just one other race suggests that there is a very good chance he will get to post. If he does, then he will not be 25/1 on the day.

In many ways the most intriguing prospect, at this early stage of the season, is **Master Minded**, with his trainer Paul Nicholls having already backed the horse at 7/1 for the King George VI Chase. Nicholls says that the horse demonstrated at Ascot and

*The powerhouse that is Denman*

Aintree last season that he stays further than two miles and so longer trips are now the way forward.

The plan is to start him at Aintree in the Old Roan Chase and then head to Kempton, after which a decision will be made on his spring target. Following Master Minded's impressive defeat of Albertas Run in the John Smith's Melling Chase at Aintree, where he was still on the bridle when moving up to challenge, Nicholls said:

"It's obvious he wants a trip now. At Cheltenham he was flat out and staying on and looking back he should have gone for the Ryanair. I train him a little differently now, working him with slower horses instead of buzzing him up."

As the former winner of two Champion Chases, Master Minded is accustomed to jumping fences more quickly than most staying horses – something which clearly stood him in good stead at Aintree. He is certainly a slicker and more reliable jumper than Long Run and at 5/1 for Kempton, as opposed to a top price of 11/8 for the Gold Cup winner, I would prefer him over the favourite.

As for Cheltenham, I am less certain of him staying the trip. He is, though, still a relatively young horse and I have no doubt that if Kauto Star is retired, and Master Minded wins or runs well in the King George, then Paul Nicholls will be keen for him to line up in the Gold Cup. The alternative would be the Ryanair Chase.

Paul Nicholls has said the Gold Cup will be the target for **What A Friend**. He says the eight-year-old needs to be "managed" – something one can glean from the fact he has run just five times since beating Money Trix in the Lexus Chase at Leopardstown in December, 2009.

What A Friend responded favourably to the first-time application of the blinkers when finishing fourth to Long Run in the Gold Cup, a performance which saw his rating rise by 10lb from 159 to 169.

What A Friend is a smooth-travelling horse at his best and he may be the type who runs well in the race for a few seasons to come.

The King George promises to be one of the highlights of the season, with **Captain Chris** expected to join Long Run and Master Minded.

*Captain Chris (left). May be even better over three miles*

The seven-year-old is a rugged, tough battler, who digs deep, rather than a cruiser like Master Minded.

This was certainly the case in the Arkle Trophy, where they always seemed to be going a stride too fast for him until the approach to the last, where his stamina came to the fore. Prone to jump right, he was wisely kept to the outside of the field by Richard Johnson before powering into the lead on the run to the final fence.

Captain Chris won in a similar manner two months later, responding bravely to Johnson's firm driving to beat Realt Dubh in the Ryanair Novices' Chase over two miles at Punchestown.

Having beaten Adams Island by 13 lengths over an extended 2m 4f in the Pendil Novices' Chase at Kempton, Captain Chris appreciated the strong pace of the Arkle and is likely to enjoy even more the three miles of the King George. Indeed, it is testament to his talent that he has been able to win twice at Grade 1 level over two miles. All will become clear after Kempton but, at this stage, he looks as if he will be ideally suited to the Gold Cup trip.

Stable-companion **Wishfull Thinking** gives owner Diana Whateley and trainer Philip Hobbs another string to their bow.

The son of Alflora indicated he was on an upward curve when beating Calgary Bay by three and a half lengths in a Grade 3 handicap chase at Cheltenham in January, equipped with a tongue-tie for the first time. He then ran second to Noble Prince in the Jewson Novices' Chase before beating Medermit by 10 lengths at Aintree and making virtually all to beat Blazing Tempo, receiving 21lb, in a 2m 5f novices' handicap chase at Punchestown in May (yielding ground).

In my view Wishfull Thinking has more speed than Captain Chris, even though the latter won his two Grade 1 races over two miles. Wishfull Thinking is certainly the more fluent jumper – Captain Chris can be rather ponderous – and it will be fascinating to learn how the two horses are going to be campaigned. The official ratings have Wishfull Thinking 4lb superior to his stable companion.

I think we can assume that one of the two will be in the line-up on Gold Cup day. At this stage I would marginally favour Captain Chris as the more likely runner, with Wishfull Thinking tackling one of the shorter races.

**Time For Rupert**, many people's idea of the Festival banker last March, finished only fifth in the RSA Chase after being found to have bled. In the rear from an early

*The up-and-coming Time For Rupert*

stage, he was never travelling and in the circumstances did very well to finish just six lengths behind the winner.

There is always a risk that horses which have bled will do so again, so caution is advised in the case of Time For Rupert. However his record at Cheltenham, the RSA apart, stands up to the closest scrutiny, with a victory and two seconds over hurdles – notably when running Big Buck's to three and a quarter lengths in the 2010 World Hurdle – and a very sound effort when beating subsequent National Hunt Chase winner Chicago Grey by eight lengths there in December. Always travelling smoothly on that occasion, he hardly touched a twig, clearing the fences with plenty to spare.

Having attained a mark of 166 over hurdles we can safely assume that Time For Rupert has the potential to improve beyond his current chase mark of 159. Current figures leave him 23lb behind Long Run, but a couple of decent pre-Christmas efforts would see him attract market interest at 16/1.

One of the most interesting contenders for the race is **Diamond Harry**.

A fragile but immensely talented horse, he has been handled with great skill and sensitivity by Nick and Jane Williams. The winner of 10 of his 13 starts, his defeats came when third to Mikael D'Haguenet in the 2009 Ballymore Novices' Hurdle and when filling the same spot behind Big Buck's in the Long Walk Hurdle at Newbury that year, and when pulled up behind Weapon's Amnesty in the 2010 RSA Chase.

The son of Sir Harry Lewis is at his best fresh – he has won on his seasonal reappearance in each of the last five seasons – and this was the case again last autumn when he beat Burton Port by one and a quarter lengths from a mark of 156 in the Hennessy. That victory saw his rating rise to 168, but he wasn't seen out again due to injuring a suspensory ligament.

Williams has always had doubts about the horse's suitability for Cheltenham, even though he has won twice there. Flatter tracks are thought to be more appropriate, while the trainer also believes the horse is better in the autumn.

Diamond Harry is clearly the type of horse who is best kept fresh for a specific target. This was even the case in his younger days, when he won a valuable bumper at Newbury on his racecourse debut in March, 2007, and was then kept back for the same race a year later. I imagine the plan this autumn will be to try and win a valuable race and then rest him with a view to having him fresh for the Gold Cup. However, given his injury and history – and the improvement he has to find – it may be best to await news from the trainer before considering a bet (20/1).

**Quito De La Roque** is worth keeping an eye on.

The winner of seven of his 11 races (second in three of the other four), the plan had been to run him at last year's Festival until trainer Colm Murphy and the owners thought better of it, switching instead to the Grade 2 Mildmay Novices' Chase at Aintree and then the Grade 1 Champion Novice Chase at Punchestown, where he took advantage of the misfortune of others.

The seven-year-old stays particularly well for a young horse but he is a slightly ponderous, deliberate, jumper at this stage of his career. On his final start at Punchestown he struggled to see a stride at some of the fences. There is, though, no denying that he has a progressive profile.

**Bostons Angel** beat Quito De La Roque by three-quarters of a length in a Grade 1 novice chase run on heavy ground over three miles at Leopardstown over Christmas. He then went on to beat Magnanimity by a head at the same track over 2m 5f in the Dr. P.J. Moriarty Novice Chase in February and then beat Jessies Dream by a neck in the RSA Chase at Cheltenham.

The seven-year-old is very tough and hard to assess because he seems to do only the minimum required to win, his trainer Jessie Harrington confirming that he has a tendency to stop when he hits the front. Bostons Angel has done enough to warrant a Gold Cup preparation but leaves the impression that conditions would need to be stamina-sapping to bring out the best of him.

**Burton Port** was retired for the season with a tendon injury following his gallant effort in the Hennessy, where he ran Diamond Harry to one and a quarter lengths. Up until then he had impressed as an extremely tough, progressive young chaser. The winner of five and second twice from seven starts over fences, he had run well to finish second to Weapon's Amnesty in the 2010 RSA Chase. Burton Port is of limited stature but he has a big heart and if Nicky Henderson can get him back to full fitness he would appeal as a possible outsider for the frame.

Of the others **Mon Parrain**, so promising last year for Paul Nicholls, and **Pandorama**, on testing ground, would merit a mention while a switch of discipline for **Big Buck's** would make life interesting.

## Conclusion

Long Run deserves to be heading the market, given his youth and potential, although doubts remain about his jumping which, though much improved, is still flawed. He has got away with it so far but, at the highest level, he cannot afford to forfeit ground and momentum through careless errors.

The up-and-coming novices from last season are headed by Time For Rupert, with Captain Chris and Wishfull Thinking also commanding great respect. Of the three I like Wishfull Thinking but, running in the same colours as Captain Chris, the latter may be deemed better suited to the race. From Ireland Quito De La Roque and Bostons Angel need to improve.

Burton Port is a tough, hardy battler but, at the risk of being accused of letting my heart rule my head, I would argue that Denman represents the value at this early stage at 25/1.

That is simply too long a price for a horse who has won the race once and finished second in it three times. Paul Nicholls and his team will be doing their utmost to ensure the horse gets to post in tip-top shape on the day and if he does, then I would expect him to start at less than half that price.

Public support alone will ensure that is the case and were he to win, the cheers will still be echoing round the Cotswolds long after the crowds have made their way back home.

# Keep informed...

By signing up for our **free newsletter** you will be eligible to receive special offers, advanced notification of publications and regular updates from Marten Julian.

You will also receive any news of horses that are available for syndication from Dark Horse Racing.

If you're online then why not register for our free monthly newsletter by visiting:

**www.martenjulian.com**

**No internet access?**
There is also a postal version available - simply call the office on 01539 741 007

# THE 2012 CHAMPION HURDLE PREVIEW

Last season's Champion Hurdle long promised to be one of the most intriguing for many years.

There were so many imponderables – would Hurricane Fly elect to run up the hill and give Montjeu his first ever winner of a race at Cheltenham? Was Oscar Whisky good enough to fill the void left by his absent stable-companion Binocular? Could Dunguib show himself to be the superstar many thought he was 12 months earlier? Was Khyber Kim able to spring a surprise? Would the trip be far enough for Peddlers Cross?

The one to start with in respect to the 2012 Champion Hurdle is the horse who did not make it to post, the 2010 winner of the race **Binocular**. It is no secret that the horse is delicate – some would probably argue that he is soft – but he is, at his best, a hugely talented performer.

Tony McCoy has handled him with great skill, appearing to accept early in a race when his mount is not 'on song'. This was certainly the case in his early runs in 2009/10 and, again, when he reappeared at Newbury last November. Travelling well between the last two flights, McCoy was easy on him as soon as it became apparent that he wasn't going to win.

Binocular looked to be back on good terms with himself next time at Kempton, landing the rescheduled Christmas Hurdle by just under four lengths from Overturn, with Starluck a couple of lengths behind in third.

Binocular could hardly have been more impressive when, in the 2010 Champion Hurdle, he stayed on well up the hill to beat Khyber Kim by three and a half lengths, with Zaynar back in third. What particularly impressed that day was the way the horse kept on so well after taking up the running approaching the second last. What has not subsequently impressed is the form of the race, with none of the 11 horses he beat building on their efforts.

*Binocular looking at his imperious best*

Those, like me, who thought there was the hint of the 'bridle horse' about him were proved wrong, with Binocular winning more in the style of a stayer than a horse who needed holding up until the last possible moment.

A link through Khyber Kim suggested that Hurricane Fly is about a stone superior to Binocular – a line of form confirmed when Hurricane Fly beat him by nine lengths in the Rabobank Champion Hurdle at Punchestown in May.

Precise plans for Binocular are uncertain this season, although the intention is to race him more regularly and aim him at the Champion Hurdle again. It will be interesting to see if his enthusiasm can be rekindled after a disappointing end to last season.

**Hurricane Fly** brought an almost flawless record to last year's Champion Hurdle, having won all but two of his 11 starts over hurdles – seven of the victories coming at Grade 1 level.

There were those who argued that four consecutive defeats of Solwhit, albeit by steadily increasing margins, didn't add up to a great deal in the context of the race. Solwhit had finished a well-beaten sixth in the 2010 Champion Hurdle but of more concern was that Hurricane Fly's sire, Montjeu, had not yet produced a horse which had won over jumps at Cheltenham – Festival or otherwise – from 44 attempts.

Hurricane Fly had, on occasions, beaten Solwhit with something in hand but at other times he had required firm driving to assert his superiority. Taking the form at face value, he came out something between 1lb and 4lb superior to Solwhit who, in turn, could be rated 12lb inferior to Binocular through the 2010 Champion Hurdle form.

Any doubts about Hurricane Fly's form, or temperament, were laid to rest on the big day. Travelling well on the inside, and jumping with great alacrity, he moved up powerfully approaching the second-last flight of hurdles and took a half-length lead over Peddlers Cross on the run to the last. It was then a question of what he would find but, to his credit, he had enough in hand to repel the renewed and determined challenge of Peddlers Cross, winning by one and a quarter lengths.

*Hurricane Fly (right) about to pounce on Peddlers Cross*

The time was two seconds slower than the Supreme Novices' Hurdle and looking back, Donald McCain's team may feel that Peddlers Cross would have appreciated his stable-companion Overturn setting a stronger pace. The steadier pace would have suited Hurricane Fly the better of the two.

Six weeks later Hurricane Fly confirmed the form with Thousand Stars and Menorah in the Rabobank Champion Hurdle at Punchestown, coming through to challenge on the bridle and winning much more easily than he had at Cheltenham.

Described as "a machine" by Ruby Walsh, Hurricane Fly again has the Champion Hurdles at Cheltenham and Punchestown as his main objectives this season. A current price of 7/4 may not appeal as great value, but if he gets a clear run through to March I could see him starting at odds-on on the day.

**Menorah** went into last year's race as the most attractive each-way bet of the race but, for the first time in his career, he finished out of the first two and came home in fifth.

He also ran a little below his best next time when fourth to Hurricane Fly at Punchestown, with the result that Philip Hobbs and the owners have decided to send him chasing. At six he is the right age for that game and he must already be on the shortlist for the Arkle Trophy. The fact that he loves Cheltenham, having won on three of his four visits to the track, will stand him in good stead.

**Dunguib**, who promised so much as a younger horse, was found to have some heat in a front leg in May so he will now miss the entire season. The plan when he returns will be to go chasing.

Plans for **Oscar Whisky** are uncertain at the moment, with connections toying between stepping him up in trip to two and a half, or even three miles, or switch to chasing.

Oscar Whisky forfeited his chance of winning the 2010 Supreme Novices' Hurdle with ill-timed mistakes, most notably at the last flight. Finishing just under four lengths behind Menorah, he looked beaten on merit.

He returned last season with an impressive and smoothly-gained seven-lengths' defeat of Any Given Day, with Celestial Halo six lengths away in third, over two and a half miles at Cheltenham. He then landed the Welsh Champion Hurdle, his target race for the season, very easily at Ffos Las before finishing third in the Champion Hurdle.

Oscar Whisky has never been a particularly fluent hurdler, and he was a little

*Oscar Whisky, who may step up in trip this season*

deliberate at a few of the flights in the Champion. This cost him momentum but he still seemed to be going well turning for home until outpaced by Hurricane Fly and Peddlers Cross on the run to the last.

The following month, stepped up to two and a half miles for the John Smith's Aintree Hurdle, he virtually reproduced his Cheltenham running to the pound with runner-up Thousand Stars. On that occasion he was kicked for home by Barry Geraghty and held on by a fast-diminishing margin to win by a neck.

Although said to show plenty of speed at home (he won a bumper over an extended 1m4f on his racecourse debut), Oscar Whisky now looks as if he requires two and a half miles. Indeed, there was a point last season when Nicky Henderson toyed with the idea of pitching him in against Big Buck's over three miles.

As for the new season, the latest news suggests Oscar Whisky's chasing career will be put on hold in favour of a campaign in staying hurdles. He will, though, have one run over the minimum trip when he will again be aimed at the Welsh Champion Hurdle, a race his owner Dai Walters is keen to try and win for the second year in succession. I would say another crack at the Champion Hurdle is unlikely.

**Khyber Kim** is a hard horse who is hard to catch right. Soundly beaten in the Champion Hurdle, he then finished way behind Big Buck's over 3m 1f at Aintree. For all his talent it would be a surprise to see him figure in this race at the age of 10. As with Mille Chief the key is to catch him fresh.

Donald McCain says that **Peddlers Cross** will now go novice chasing.

I was a little surprised by this because had last year's Champion Hurdle been a more strongly-run race he might have got the better of Hurricane Fly. As it was there was only one and a quarter lengths between them, while I am prepared to overlook his final effort at Aintree because he was found to be wrong after the race.

Peddlers Cross has a tenacious way of racing. He is a battler more than a cruiser, who stays every yard of the trip as you would expect from a horse who won an Irish point-to-point and at championship level over 2m 5f as a novice.

*Peddlers Cross, who may now be switched to chasing*

Peddlers Cross has sometimes left his trainer swooning at the quality of his work, comparing it to some of the gallops he witnessed from Group-class performers when he was employed during his earlier years by Luca Cumani.

The horse is a quick jumper of hurdles – he impressed particularly in this regard, despite hating the ground, at Kelso – and we know the hill holds no terrors for him. McCain says the horse's main target is more likely to be the Arkle Chase than the RSA. Things now appear to be decided but if, for some reason, Peddlers Cross struggled over fences, or something were to happen to Hurricane Fly, then don't be surprised if they redirect Peddlers Cross to hurdles.

One of the most exciting novice hurdlers from last season is probably **Spirit Son**.

The son of Poliglote won a hurdle race on his sole start in France and then impressed when winning twice in novice company at Huntingdon and Exeter. He was well supported for the Supreme Novices' Hurdle and duly went close, travelling comfortably just a couple of lengths off the pace and staying on strongly after the last to chase home Al Ferof, pulling over three lengths clear of stable-companion Sprinter Sacre, with Cue Card back in fourth.

*Spirit Son, up with the pick of last season's novice hurdlers*

He then appeared at Aintree, taking on Cue Card again in the 2m 4f John Smith's Mersey Novices' Hurdle, and came clear to beat him by 13 lengths, with Rock On Ruby eight lengths away in third.

Nicky Henderson was impressed, saying afterwards:

"Cheltenham probably came six months early and I promise you he has massive scope for improvement. Barry says he is just getting the right feel off him and he will certainly be trained as a hurdler, not a novice chaser, next season."

With slight doubts about the reliability of Binocular and Oscar Whisky set to follow the staying hurdling route, Spirit Son is probably a sensible long-term proposition at 10/1 for the Champion Hurdle. It will stand him in good stead that he has won over two and a half miles and having run just four times over hurdles it is easy to see why connections feel there is more improvement to come from him.

**Grandouet** earned the reward for good efforts in the Triumph Hurdle, where he finished third, and Aintree, where he was brought down when travelling well at the second last, when beating Kumbeshwar by nine lengths in the AES Champion 4YO Hurdle at Punchestown in May.

He beat the second much more easily than Zarkandar did at Aintree, but after winning Barry Geraghty suggested the horse should go chasing this season. At the time of writing I am unaware of the trainer's plans, but in my opinion he was close enough to the top of the juvenile hurdling tree to warrant another season over hurdles.

Paul Nicholls says that he will be training **Zarkandar** for the Champion Hurdle. A winner, second and third from three starts on the Flat in France, he surprised his trainer when making a winning hurdling debut at Kempton in February before battling on bravely to win the Triumph Hurdle, very much in the manner of a stayer. He won in a similarly workmanlike manner when beating Kumbeshwar by one and a quarter lengths next time in a Grade 1 event at Aintree.

Afterwards Paul Nicholls said the horse may not have been at his best, having had a mouth abscess which required treatment a week earlier. Also, it is worth noting that Zarkandar wore blinkers on each of his three starts on the Flat in France and they may well be reapplied at some point this season. After winning at Cheltenham Nicholls said:

"I think he could win the Champion Hurdle next season. When I bought him I loved

*Zarkandar, rated a serious Champion Hurdle prospect by his trainer*

him, but he was coltish and badly behaved. I thought he might finish in the first four at Kempton and the plan was to put him away for the season, but he astounded me. He has obviously got that bit of class and with another summer he could be anything. He would have killed you if he could, but since we had him gelded he is like your best mate."

Zarkandar has had a wind operation since last season and may well start the new campaign in the Greatwood Hurdle at Cheltenham. His trainer's confidence is compelling even though, visually, the horse does not impress.

**Al Ferof** is featured in some lists for the Champion Hurdle but Paul Nicholls says the plan is to send him novice chasing.

It remains to be seen if we will see **Rite Of Passage** this season. Trainer Dermot Weld has already said the horse will be out of action for the remainder of 2011, so the chances of a return this season look slim.

**Unaccompanied**, also trained by Weld, ran very well to finish second to Zarkandar in the Triumph Hurdle and then won a 1m 2f Listed contest on the Flat at the Curragh in April (St Nicholas Abbey was back in third). A month later she finished a long way behind Grandouet at Punchestown.

Unaccompanied might possibly have finished closer to the winner at Cheltenham had she not had to be switched after getting squeezed approaching the last flight of hurdles.

A big filly with a touch of class, don't be surprised to see this daughter of Danehill Dancer have a good season. She comes out just a few pounds behind Zarkandar on her Cheltenham running yet currently stands at around three times the price (33/1).

I nominate Unaccompanied as the most interesting of the long-priced contenders for the 2012 Champion Hurdle

**The Real Article** needs watching.

*Unaccompanied – a talented mare with a touch of class*

Edward O'Grady's six-year-old was unbeaten in three summer bumpers in 2010 before switching to hurdles, winning once and running a short-head second to Captain Cee Bee in a Grade 3 event at Tipperary this July. He has since won a flat race at Wexford and a Grade 2 hurdle at Tipperary, beating Luska Lad by eight lengths. The trainer says the horse wasn't able to take on the top novices last season because he "wasn't right."

## Conclusion

Hurricane Fly is the type of horse who will appreciate a quiet build-up to the Champion Hurdle. A horse with an immense amount of class, and a few gears to boot, if everything goes according to plan he may well start an odds-on chance on the day.

Spirit Son represents fair value at 10/1 given that he, too, has the race as his main objective. Zarkandar may improve, possibly for the application of headgear, but from last year's juveniles I prefer Dermot Weld's mare Unaccompanied. Few hurdlers have the class to win a mile and a quarter Listed race on the Flat and, her last run apart, she showed progressive form last season.

Binocular would look very big value at the current 14/1 if he were to run up to his best in the pre-Cheltenham trials, while a switch back to hurdling for Peddlers Cross would definitely cause a shake-up in the markets.

Hurricane Fly is a worthy favourite but, for value, the one I recommend is Unaccompanied at 33/1. My hope is that her able trainer decides to aim her at the race.

# Keep informed...

By signing up for our **free newsletter** you will be eligible to receive special offers, advanced notification of publications and regular updates from Marten Julian.

You will also receive any news of horses that are available for syndication from Dark Horse Racing.

If you're online then why not register for our free monthly newsletter by visiting:

## www.martenjulian.com

**No internet access?**
There is also a postal version available - simply call the office on 01539 741 007

# THE 2012 QUEEN MOTHER CHAMPION CHASE PREVIEW

The early favourite for the 2012 Queen Mother Champion Chase is **Sizing Europe**, winner of the 2010 Arkle Trophy by three-quarters of a length from Somersby and then again in this race at the Festival last year, when he beat Big Zeb by five lengths.

Next time out Big Zeb reversed that form, beating him by three-quarters of a length in the Grade 1 Boylesports.com Champion Chase at Punchestown.

*Sizing Europe, who has never fallen over fences*

The son of Pistolet Bleu did not impress on his return to action at Gowran Park in October, making a series of mistakes and all out to beat a rival rated 40lb his inferior. It would be wrong to judge him on that performance as his overall record reads impressively, with seven victories, three seconds and two thirds from his last 12 outings – most of them at a high level. Sizing Europe is a horse who puts a lot into his races, racing prominently and not always jumping cleanly. Yet he has never fallen over fences, and has never finished out of the first three.

Wherever Sizing Europe is you can be sure that **Big Zeb** is never that far away.

The 10-year-old has finished either first or second in his last seven starts, and after chasing home Sizing Europe in this race last year he reversed the form when they met again at Punchestown. He is a regular here and won this race in 2010 by six lengths from Forpadydeplasterer, having fallen in the 2009 running won by Master Minded.

*Big Zeb – so reliable and consistent at the highest level*

*Finian's Rainbow – a contender for the highest honours over two miles*

**Finian's Rainbow** looks a natural for this race.

The eight-year-old won over two and a half miles as a hurdler, but two miles is definitely his trip and he ran a stormer behind Captain Chris in the Arkle here last spring before making all to beat Ghizao in the John Smith's Maghull Novices' Chase at Aintree. It should be said that Finian's Rainbow has a tendency to get low at a few of his fences, but he also put in some excellent leaps in the Arkle – notably at the open ditch - and appeared to be going better than ultimate winner Captain Chris turning for home until the latter's stamina came to his aid.

Finian's Rainbow was probably unsuited to sharing the pacemaking role with Stagecoach Pearl and Dan Breen in the Arkle but the way he powered away on the turn for home, as he did next time out between the last two fences at Aintree, established that this is a horse with a great deal of class.

**Captain Chris** does not have the pace of Finian's Rainbow but, as we saw at Cheltenham and then Punchestown, he is a very tough horse who can call upon deep reserves of stamina. There are no more than a few pounds between the two, and it may be that connections opt to aim instead at the Gold Cup. I expect their decision will be influenced by how the main contenders perform, with special reference to stable-companion Wishfull Thinking.

**Ghizao** ties in with last season's top 2m novice form.

Paul Nicholls has always left the impression that the son of Tiger Hill has more to offer than we have so far seen but having beaten Captain Chris by 10 lengths at Cheltenham in November, he forfeited any chance of confirming that form in the Arkle due to a couple of serious mistakes. He was seen in a better light when running Finian's Rainbow to a couple of lengths at Aintree, but there again a blunder two out cost him momentum at a critical time.

Ghizao may have more scope for improvement than a few of these but my concern is that he has tended to fall short on the big occasion. His jumping remains a concern.

**Master Minded**, winner of this race in 2008 and 2009, is now being aimed at a programme over two and a half miles and, perhaps, further. There is always the chance he may revert to two miles for this race, but if he runs well in the King George VI Chase on Boxing Day then the Gold Cup would be more likely to come under consideration.

**Noble Prince** could enter the reckoning. Paul Nolan's son of Montjeu gave the sire his second winner at Cheltenham when beating Wishfull Thinking by four lengths in the Jewson Novices' Chase over two and a half miles. He then fell when looking a danger behind Realt Dubh at Fairyhouse.

Noble Prince was a fair performer over hurdles and with just five runs over fences there may be more improvement to come. He did well to pass Wishfull Thinking after the last in the Jewson as the runner-up was travelling powerfully at the time. The horse's form over two and a half miles – four of his five victories under Rules have been at that trip – will stand him in good stead. However the Ryanair Chase, over 2m 5f, is probably the more likely target for him.

**Realt Dubh** has almost nine lengths to find with Captain Chris on Arkle form. He then went to Fairyhouse, beating Loosen My Load by 11 lengths, before making up

*Master Minded – a potent force at his best*

seven and a half of the nine lengths' deficit with Captain Chris at Punchestown.

Two earlier defeats of Noble Prince, both at Leopardstown, entitle him to serious consideration in the context of this race and Paul Carberry's patient style of riding seems to suit the horse.

**Captain Cee Bee** is a regular at the meeting but at the last two Festivals he has been soundly beaten by Sizing Europe and, as an 11-year-old next March, he is unlikely to be getting any better.

## Conclusion

The horse which most excites me for this race is Finian's Rainbow. That surge he produced to go clear on the descent to the final bend in last year's Arkle left a lasting impression, even though he was subsequently outstayed on the run to the line. Finian's Rainbow has the courage to match his talent and, as was the case with Long Run, I would expect Nicky Henderson and his team to work on improving the horse's jumping technique.

Sizing Europe and Big Zeb are likely to play their part again, while Captain Chris has to enter calculations if this is the route his connections decide to take. However the one which I'll be watching closely, mindful that the Ryanair may appeal more, is Noble Prince. I feel that we have yet to see the best of him.

There is little doubt, with connections having decided two miles is his trip, that Finian's Rainbow will be aimed specifically at the Queen Mother Champion Chase. This makes the current 8/1 a reasonable long-term investment, with the prospect of trading should the price shorten.

# A LAKELAND DREAM

*It is my intention to follow the progress of the yearling colt named Samoset in forthcoming Dark Horse Annuals, starting here with his background and the aspirations his owners have for him.*

Maurice Chapman, best known in racing circles as the owner of Chief Dan George, has achieved a great deal in his life.

Furthermore, it does not appear to have taken much out of him. At 71, he could quite easily pass for a man 20 years younger.

Brought up and educated at Barrow Grammar School, he worked with Shell and then moved on to Proctor and Gamble. A gifted sportsman – he captained Crewe and Nantwich RU Club – he decided to move on to an advertising agency in London and was given the role of managing the lucrative and substantial Co-operative account.

A three-year stint in Bermuda, working with the Minister of Tourism Henry Vesey, enabled him to pursue his interests in sport before he returned to live at Millom, where he set up and developed a site with holiday chalet homes. He sold that and with the proceeds bought the Acrastyle engineering company in Ulverston, despite knowing precious little about the subject matter.

There for 24 years, he focused his energies on exports, which rose from zero when he started to over £50 million – an achievement which was recognised in 1986 with the award of an MBE, although Maurice is endearingly vague about the precise reason why he got it.

He delights in talking about those days. He travelled the world plying his trade, installing sub-stations in Ecuador and doing business in Hong Kong, China, Vietnam, Paraguay, Colombia and Japan.

Yet throughout those travels his love of animals remained constant. His father Bill rode laundry horses to and from work, while the family later had pigs and ponies. When he left Acrastyle in the late 90s he acquired two farms in the Scottish Borders, with over 1,200 sheep, 100 cattle and, of course, horses.

He showed me, with pride, the pictures of his prize-winning bulls, which included a supreme champion at both the Royal Highland Show and the Royal Lancashire Show.

*True North, who did so well for Maurice*

When he moved back to the Lakes he bought a horse, True North, who he still looks after at home.

But it is Chief Dan George with whom he has been most closely linked.

The 11-year-old has done him proud, winning almost £200,000 in prize money and nine races including the Grade 1 Sefton Novices' Hurdle at Aintree and, most famously, the William Hill Trophy Handicap at the 2010 Cheltenham Festival. There, under a tremendous ride from Paddy Aspell, he just held the power-packed finish of Timmy Murphy, riding The Package for the mighty Pipe yard.

There are hopes that Chief Dan George, named after an Indian chief, will be in action again this season, but Maurice and his racing partner Arnold Headdock are looking further ahead.

We all have dreams, more so than most in racing, and Arnold had a proper old-fashioned one.

He actually dreamt that he both owned, and bred, a Derby winner.

So he and Maurice went around a few of the country's leading studs to find a sire for Arnold's mare, Great Quest.

Great Quest was bred for great things.

A daughter of Montjeu, she started life with Tommy Stack in 2005 and was placed

*Chief Dan George*

a few times before winning a modest 2m 1f handicap at Killarney in July, 2006. That proved to be her only success from 30 starts, six of them over hurdles, but as a Montjeu mare she warranted a good mate although it was pure chance that they decided to go for Sir Percy.

"Arnold was walking past the paddock at the stud when Sir Percy bounded up to him. Arnold took that as a sign, believing he was the special one, so that was that. Great Quest was going to visit Sir Percy."

The result has been a lovely, scopey young colt who would probably have found a pitch at one of the autumn's top sales had Maurice and Arnold so wished. But that was not the intention because they want to keep him to race for themselves, starting as a two-year-old next season.

*Maurice with Samoset*

However quirky the reasons for choosing Sir Percy, subsequent events would suggest Arnold has gifts of foresight and prescience which would earn him a small fortune if he were to set up camp with the gypsy fortune tellers at Epsom on Derby day.

The Dewhurst winner and 2006 Derby winner has made a brilliant start at stud, with a dozen or so winners including the Listed placed Percy Jackson, dual-winner Cavaleiro and David Elsworth's Salford Art.

It can now be confidently assumed that Sir Percy will make it as a sire, especially after a yearling out of Bombazine – from a line nurtured by the late Gerald Leigh – fetched 260,000gns this autumn, to follow his top priced 80,000gns yearling in 2010.

Keeping with the Indian theme, which started with Chief Dan George, Maurice and Arnold have decided to name their colt Samoset.

"Samoset was the first native American to make contact with the Pilgrim Fathers, who were more than a little surprised when he turned up one day and strolled through the middle of their encampment to greet them in broken English. He was a member of the Wompanoag tribe and he had learned the language from some English fishermen who had arrived in what is now recognised as Maine."

It has been noted over the years that most good horses have good names. Samoset is a good name.

The horse has a Derby pedigree, with some of the stud book's top sires – Darshaan, Mark Of Esteem, Montjeu, Shernazar and Sadler's Wells – all within three generations of him.

Finally, there is a saying that it is better to be born lucky than rich. I think we can safely say both Maurice and Arnold have been lucky.

As somebody once said, nothing happens unless first we dream. Let's wish Maurice and Arnold every good fortune as they embark on their journey.

# CHELTENHAM FESTIVAL 2012 PRICES

## 2012 CHELTENHAM GOLD CUP

| | Sky Bet | Totesport | Betfred | Victor Chandler | Paddy Power | Ladbrokes | Coral | William Hill |
|---|---|---|---|---|---|---|---|---|
| Long Run | 5/2 | 5/2 | 5/2 | 9/4 | 2/1 | 5/2 | 9/4 | 5/2 |
| Time For Rupert | 16/1 | 12/1 | 12/1 | 14/1 | 16/1 | 14/1 | 12/1 | 16/1 |
| Captain Chris 14/1 | 16/1 | 16/1 | 16/1 | 16/1 | 16/1 | 14/1 | 14/1 | |
| Master Minded | 16/1 | 20/1 | 16/1 | 16/1 | 14/1 | 14/1 | | |
| Diamond Harry | 16/1 | 16/1 | 16/1 | 20/1 | 16/1 | 20/1 | 20/1 | 16/1 |
| Wishfull Thinking | 20/1 | 20/1 | 16/1 | 16/1 | 14/1 | | | |
| Quito De La Roque | 20/1 | 20/1 | 20/1 | 16/1 | 16/1 | 25/1 | 20/1 | 25/1 |
| Bostons Angel | 25/1 | 16/1 | 25/1 | 25/1 | 25/1 | 25/1 | | |
| Denman | 20/1 | 20/1 | 20/1 | 25/1 | 20/1 | 20/1 | 14/1 | |
| Big Bucks | | | | | | | | |
| Bensalem | 25/1 | | | | | | | |
| Rubi Ball | 16/1 | | | | | | | |
| Mid Dancer | | | | | | | | |
| Burton Port | 20/1 | 16/1 | 16/1 | 20/1 | 20/1 | | | |
| Sizing Europe | 33/1 | | | | | | | |
| Michel Le Bon | 33/1 | | | | | | | |
| Albertas Run | | | | | | | | |
| Punchestowns | | | | | | | | |
| Jessies Dream | 20/1 | 33/1 | 25/1 | 40/1 | 33/1 | 33/1 | | |
| Rubi Light | 33/1 | 25/1 | 33/1 | 40/1 | | | | |
| Somersby | 40/1 | | | | | | | |
| Mon Parrain | 25/1 | 25/1 | 25/1 | 33/1 | 33/1 | 25/1 | | |
| Pandorama | 33/1 | 33/1 | 25/1 | | | | | |
| Kauto Star | 33/1 | | | | | | | |
| Riverside Theatre | 20/1 | 25/1 | 16/1 | 16/1 | | | | |
| What A Friend | 25/1 | 33/1 | 40/1 | 33/1 | | | | |
| Chicago Grey | 33/1 | 40/1 | | | | | | |
| Grands Crus | | | | | | | | |
| Wayward Prince | 40/1 | 33/1 | 33/1 | 33/1 | | | | |
| Aiteen Thirtythree | 50/1 | | | | | | | |
| Weird Al | 33/1 | | | | | | | |
| Kempes | 50/1 | 33/1 | | | | | | |
| First Lieutenant | | | | | | | | |
| Master Of The Hall | 50/1 | | | | | | | |

| | Sky Bet | Totesport | Betfred | Victor Chandler | Paddy Power | Ladbrokes | Coral | William Hill |
|---|---|---|---|---|---|---|---|---|
| The Giant Bolster | 50/1 | | | | | | | |
| Poquelin | 33/1 | | | | | | | |
| Mikael DHaguenet | 50/1 | | | | | | | |
| Midnight Chase | 50/1 | 50/1 | | | | | | |
| Noble Prince | 33/1 | 25/1 | 33/1 | 25/1 | | | | |
| Wymott | 33/1 | | | | | | | |
| China Rock | 66/1 | 33/1 | | | | | | |
| Neptune Collonges | 66/1 | | | | | | | |
| Forpadydeplasterer | 100/1 | | | | | | | |
| Imperial Commander | | | | | | | | |

## 2012 CHAMPION HURDLE

| | Sky Bet | Totesport | Betfred | Victor Chandler | Paddy Power | Ladbrokes | Coral | William Hill |
|---|---|---|---|---|---|---|---|---|
| Hurricane Fly | 6/4 | 7/4 | 7/4 | 6/4 | 7/4 | 7/4 | 7/4 | 13/8 |
| Spirit Son | 9/1 | 8/1 | 8/1 | 8/1 | 10/1 | 10/1 | 8/1 | 8/1 |
| Zarkandar | 10/1 | 10/1 | 10/1 | 10/1 | 12/1 | 10/1 | 12/1 | 10/1 |
| Binocular | 12/1 | 10/1 | 10/1 | 14/1 | 12/1 | 10/1 | 12/1 | 12/1 |
| Oscars Well | 14/1 | 20/1 | 20/1 | 16/1 | 16/1 | 16/1 | 14/1 | 16/1 |
| Peddlers Cross | | 14/1 | 14/1 | 10/1 | 12/1 | | 8/1 | 7/1 |
| Rite Of Passage | | | | 20/1 | | | | |
| The Real Article | 25/1 | 25/1 | 25/1 | 20/1 | 25/1 | 25/1 | 20/1 | 25/1 |
| Grandouet | 20/1 | 16/1 | 16/1 | 16/1 | 25/1 | 20/1 | 16/1 | 20/1 |
| Al Ferof | 20/1 | 14/1 | 14/1 | 14/1 | 25/1 | | 10/1 | |
| Pittoni | | | | | | | | |
| Oscar Whisky | 25/1 | 14/1 | 14/1 | 14/1 | 20/1 | 14/1 | 16/1 | 16/1 |
| Unaccompanied | 33/1 | | 25/1 | 33/1 | 25/1 | | | 33/1 |
| Casual Conquest | | | | 25/1 | | | | |
| Topolski | | | | 33/1 | 33/1 | 33/1 | 25/1 | |
| Final Approach | | | | 33/1 | | | | |
| Menorah | 33/1 | 16/1 | 16/1 | 16/1 | 25/1 | | 20/1 | 16/1 |
| Thousand Stars | 33/1 | 14/1 | 14/1 | 33/1 | | | | 33/1 |
| Zaidpour | | | | 33/1 | | | | 33/1 |
| Overturn | | | | 33/1 | | | | |
| Roi Du Val | | | | | | | | |
| Sanctuaire | | | | 40/1 | | | | |
| Go Native | | | | 50/1 | | | | |
| So Young | 50/1 | | | 25/1 | 25/1 | | 25/1 | |
| Rock On Ruby | | | | 50/1 | | | | |
| Cue Card | 50/1 | 25/1 | 25/1 | 33/1 | | | 25/1 | 20/1 |
| Recession Proof | | | | 50/1 | | | | |
| Shot From The Hip | | | | | | | | |
| Get Me Out Of Here | | | | 40/1 | | | | |
| Dunguib | | | | 25/1 | | | | |
| Sprinter Sacre | 33/1 | 20/1 | 20/1 | 20/1 | 25/1 | | | |
| Kumbeshwar | 50/1 | | | 50/1 | | | | 33/1 |
| Prince Of Pirates | | | | 33/1 | | | | |
| Soldatino | | | | 50/1 | | | | |
| Alaivan | | | | 50/1 | | | | |
| Black And Bent | | | | | | | 50/1 | |
| Sam Winner | 50/1 | | | 33/1 | | | | |
| Dandino | | | | | | 40/1 | | 66/1 |
| Kid Cassidy | | | | 40/1 | | | | |
| Clerks Choice | | | | 66/1 | | | | |
| Khyber Kim | 66/1 | | | 25/1 | | | | |

| | Sky Bet | Totesport | Betfred | Victor Chandler | Paddy Power | Ladbrokes | Coral | William Hill |
|---|---|---|---|---|---|---|---|---|
| Brampour | | | | 66/1 | | | | |
| Third Intention | | | | 100/1 | | | | |
| A Media Luz | | | | 66/1 | | | | |
| Palawi | | | | 150/1 | | | | |
| Kalann | | | | | | | | |
| Moon Dice | | | | | | | | |
| Hildisvini | | | | | | | | |
| Starluck | | | | | | | | |
| Chablais | | | | | | | | |
| Quevega | | | | | | | | |
| Tocca Ferro | | | | | | | | |
| Australia Day | | | | | | | | |
| Solwhit | | | | | | | | |
| Smad Place | | | | | | | | |
| What A Charm | | | | | | | | |
| Minella Class | | | | | | | | |
| Marsh Warbler | | | | | | | | |
| Molotof | | | | | | | | |
| Houblon Des Obeaux | | | | | | | | |

## 2012 QUEEN MOTHER CHAMPION CHASE

| | Sky Bet | Totesport | Betfred | Victor Chandler | Paddy Power | Ladbrokes | Coral | William Hill |
|---|---|---|---|---|---|---|---|---|
| Sizing Europe | 9/2 | 5/1 | 5/1 | 5/1 | 4/1 | 5/1 | 4/1 | 4/1 |
| Finians Rainbow | 8/1 | 8/1 | 8/1 | 7/1 | 8/1 | 8/1 | 8/1 | 8/1 |
| Big Zeb | 6/1 | 13/2 | 13/2 | 5/1 | 6/1 | 6/1 | 6/1 | 6/1 |
| Captain Chris | 8/1 | 9/1 | 9/1 | 8/1 | 12/1 | 8/1 | 8/1 | 10/1 |
| Master Minded | 16/1 | 10/1 | 10/1 | 16/1 | 8/1 | 10/1 | 10/1 | |
| Noble Prince | 14/1 | 12/1 | 14/1 | 14/1 | | | | |
| Ghizao | 14/1 | 18/1 | 18/1 | 16/1 | 14/1 | 16/1 | 20/1 | |
| Realt Dubh | 16/1 | 16/1 | 16/1 | 16/1 | 16/1 | 16/1 | 16/1 | 20/1 |
| Wishful Thinking | 25/1 | | | | | | | |
| Medermit | 25/1 | 16/1 | 14/1 | 14/1 | | | | |
| Royal Charm | 25/1 | | | | | | | |
| Flat Out | 33/1 | | | | | | | |
| Captain Cee Bee | 25/1 | 25/1 | 25/1 | 20/1 | 20/1 | 20/1 | 16/1 | |
| Crack Away Jack | 33/1 | 25/1 | | | | | | |
| Somersby | 33/1 | 33/1 | | | | | | |
| French Opera | 25/1 | 33/1 | 25/1 | | | | | |
| Mon Parrain | | | | | | | | |
| Golden Silver | 28/1 | 33/1 | 33/1 | 25/1 | 20/1 | | | |
| Tataniano | 33/1 | 40/1 | | | | | | |
| Dan Breen | 40/1 | | | | | | | |
| Go Native | 33/1 | | | | | | | |
| Mamlook | 40/1 | | | | | | | |
| Mikael DHaguenet | 40/1 | | | | | | | |
| Forpadydeplasterer | | | | | | | | |
| Punchestowns | | | | | | | | |
| Woolcombe Folly | 33/1 | 25/1 | | | | | | |
| Barker | 66/1 | | | | | | | |
| Rock Noir | 66/1 | | | | | | | |
| Al Ferof | | | | | | | | |
| Cue Card | | | | | | | | |
| Peddlers Cross | | | | | | | | |
| Sprinter Sacre | | | | | | | | |
| Kauto Stone | | | | | | | | |
| West With The Wind | | | | | | | | |

# INDEX